JAMES BALDWIN

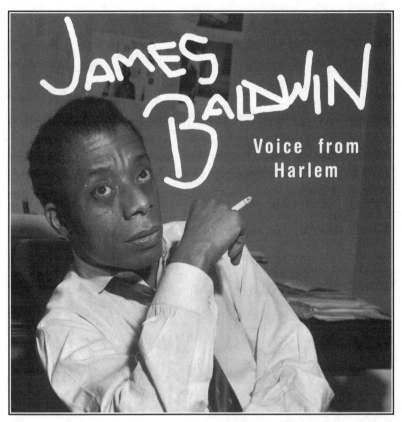

JAMES BALDWIN
Voice from Harlem

by Ted Gottfried

An Impact Biography

Franklin Watts
A Division of Grolier Publishing

New York   London   Hong Kong   Sydney
Danbury, Connecticut

FLOCA

In memory of Robert P. Mills—"Bob"—who as literary agent to James Baldwin and this author never failed to put his clients first, and to act with courtesy and an integrity which set the highest standards for his profession.

Photographs ©: AP/Wide World Photos: 25, 59, 62, 77, 78,91, 97, 98; Archive Photos: 87, 93, 65; Corbis-Bettmann: 21, 35, 43; Reuters/Corbis-Bettmann: 10; UPI/Corbis-Bettmann: cover, 3, 16, 22, 31, 42, 71, 72, 75.

Library of Congress Cataloging-in Publication Data

Gottfried, Ted
    James Baldwin: voice from Harlem / Ted Gottfried.
        p. cm. — (An Impact biography)
    Includes bibliographical references and index.
    ISBN 0-531-11318-3 (lib. bdg.)   0-531-15863-2 (pbk.)
    1. Baldwin, James, 1924-1987—Juvenile literature. 2. Afro-American authors—20th century—Biography—Juvenile literature.
3. Civil rights workers—United States—Biography—Juvenile literature.
4. Gay men—United States—Biography—Juvenile literature. 5. Harlem (New York, N.Y.)—Biography—Juvenile literature. I. Title.
PS3552.A45Z66 1997
818'.5409—dc20
[B]   96-18965
                                               CIP
                                             AC

1 2 3 4 5 6 7 8 9 10 R 06 05 04 03 02 01 00 99 98 97

Contents

One	Love One, Love All	9
Two	Library and Church: Books and Lessons	15
Three	Goodbye to Harlem	28
Four	Paris	40
Five	Lucien and "Giovanni's Room"	46
Six	The Civil Rights Struggle	55
Seven	"Another Country"	64
Eight	"The Fire Next Time"	70
Nine	Caught in the Middle	80
Ten	"Precious Lord, Take My Hand"	89

Source notes	99
Books by James Baldwin	106
Index	109

Acknowledgments

For their help in accessing research for this book, many thanks to those in the New York Office of the National Urban League, personnel at Hampshire College and the University of Massachusetts, and at the Countee Cullen and Mid-Manhattan branches of the New York Public Library, as well as the Central Research Library, and the central branch of the Queensboro Public Library. Thanks is also due to the staff of the National Coalition Against Censorship.

I am grateful for the cooperation of my editor, E. Russell Primm III, and for the never-failing support of my friend Janet Bode. And once again I want to acknowledge with much love the contribution of my wife, Harriet Gottfried, who—as always—read and critiqued each chapter of this book as it was written.

O N E

Love One, Love All

Many children, when they are young, think badly of themselves. They look around them and see people— children and adults—who seem smarter, stronger, richer, better-looking than they are. The world is big and they are small, and the odds against them seem too great to overcome. They feel inferior.

This is called low self-image. James Baldwin, a black man who became one of America's greatest writers, suffered from it when he was young. In some ways the story of his life is the story of how he overcame it.

He was born to an unmarried mother at a time when the "sins" of the parents were widely believed to permanently scar the character of the child. Throughout childhood and as an adult James was short and skinny—underweight. He wasn't very strong, and he wasn't very good at sports. His eyes bulged in his thin brown face and his high forehead was wrinkled like a bulldog's. His stepfather called him the ugliest child he had ever seen, and once when James was five or six years old, he ran upstairs to report that he had seen an old, drunken woman in the street "uglier than me."[1]

James was a black child at a time and in a country where legal segregation still existed and racial discrimination was a daily fact of life for

James Baldwin reads his autobiographical novel:
Go Tell It on the Mountain.

African Americans. As he grew older, he realized that he was different from the mainstream in another way. He was gay—or, more accurately, bisexual. He was attracted to women, but he was more strongly attracted to men.

Always, James Baldwin embraced being black. As he grew older, he accepted his sexual feelings toward men. Doing so, he accepted himself.

What matter if he was small and scrawny and had eyes like a frog? Accepting himself, he accepted his flaws and his strong points as well. In his first book, the autobiographical novel *Go Tell It on the Mountain,* he wrote about being a child who was "ugly, who was always the smallest boy in his class, and who had no friends,"[2] only to recognize one day that "he had in himself a power that other people lacked; that he could use this to save himself, to raise himself."[3]

His white teachers said he was smart. As a boy he demonstrated a gift for expressing himself and for swaying other people. He embraced this ability and at age fourteen he began preaching in a small church in New York City's Harlem. Black adults thought he might become something great.

James took pride in his intelligence, in being able to learn and express himself, in his power as a speaker and his ability to move people. He discovered he could write as well as speak. In his writing he would "tell it like it is," and this would offend some people, black and white, and make them angry. But from the first he hoped his writing might make people see what they had not seen before, persuade them toward an understanding they had lacked, and perhaps change the world ever so slightly for the better.

His journey was filled with struggle, and it had many pitfalls and disappointments. Success brought no real relief from prejudice. Failure was often bitter and plunged him into depression. The ongoing persecution of African Americans sometimes pushed him into despair.

His second novel, *Giovanni's Room*, was written in Paris following a period of financial hardship, unhappy relationships, and rejection. It was a tragic tale about a gay young white American who cannot accept his true nature. Its publication meant that James Baldwin had in effect admitted he was gay; he had come out of the closet. At this time, the 1950s, only a few major American authors had written about their homosexuality. Most who were gay had not.

Some African Americans had been offended by Baldwin's harsh portrait of the black community in *Go Tell It on the Mountain*. Now others who had regarded that book and his essays on racial discrimination positively and who had regarded Baldwin as a spokesperson for African Americans, were appalled that *Giovanni's Room* not only ignored the question of race but also revealed their champion as a homosexual. To be black had always been to be vulnerable; to be gay in the 1950s was at best to be considered a comic figure and at worst to be regarded as a pervert. How could such a person speak for the black community?

Yet the day would come when James Baldwin would speak for African Americans so truly that it would lift their spirits at the same time that it exposed the depth of their bitterness. Then it would not be American blacks, but whites, who would draw back and object that his words were exaggerations. The cause of their protests was a book-length essay called *The Fire Next Time*. The furious debate it ignited, however, was immediate.

The work dealt with the Black Muslim movement headed by Elijah Muhammad and Malcolm X and detailed the ongoing oppression that gave rise to Black Muslim demands that American blacks separate themselves from American whites. Baldwin didn't believe in separating, but he thought the problems behind the demands were very real and that they were not being faced by white people. "It is galling indeed," he wrote, "to have stood so long, hat in hand, waiting for [white] Americans to grow up enough to realize that [blacks] do not threaten them."[4]

The Fire Next Time regarded some whites as cruel beyond belief in their treatment of blacks (segregation, discrimination, police brutality, lynchings, etc.) and others as willing to ignore what whites did to blacks every day even as they profited by it. Baldwin was writing in the early 1960s when the civil rights movement was at its peak, when black children were killed in church bombings and southern police were turning fire hoses and dogs on black protesters. He was writing at a time when well-meaning whites and blacks were fighting for integration. And he was explaining that the Black Muslims did not want integration because they believed that the treatment of blacks by whites had doomed the white race.

"Do I really *want* to be integrated into a burning house?" was the question Baldwin raised.[5] And he warned of "historical vengeance, a cosmic vengeance, based on the law that we recognize when we say, 'Whatever goes up must come down.'"[6] He warned that while black people might never be able to achieve their fair share of power in the United States, "they are very well placed to precipitate chaos and bring down the curtain on the American dream."[7]

Some people thought that Baldwin's grasp of the consequences of ignoring the limits to black patience meant that he approved a violent course of action. The whites who identified him with the views of the Black Muslims were blind to his specific rejection of it in *The Fire Next Time.* "I am very much concerned that American Negroes achieve their freedom here in the United States," he wrote. "But I am also concerned for their dignity, for the health of their souls, and must oppose any attempt that Negroes may make to do to others what has been done to them."[8]

Still, many white people missed the point. They thought *The Fire Next Time* was about justifying extremist black people to white people. It wasn't. It was about explaining the corner into which whites had pushed American blacks. It was about chickens coming home to roost.

James Baldwin's main concern was black people, but he knew about white people as well. He didn't hate them, but he thought they were sleepwalking. He was a prophet and he saw the future and it was terrible to behold. He saw the race riots to come. He saw Watts and Newark and Detroit, Crown Heights and Los Angeles and Boston. He saw the unleashing of violence which, while not acceptable to most blacks, would seem to some to be the only course open.

Whatever our race, we live with his vision today. But we have forgotten his main message.

James Baldwin's message is love. It is at the core of everything he wrote—novels, nonfiction, plays, articles, film criticism—everything. He understood that white people have many things to teach black people and that this education was important to young African Americans, but he believed that when it came to love, blacks should be the teachers because they had much to offer whites in the way of lessons about love.

The ultimate love, as Baldwin saw it, is the love one can summon up toward the person who is hurting you, holding you down, persecuting you. It is the love that inspires forgiveness for the weakness that makes a person a bully. Blacks, he told whites, have had to "bear you, and sometimes even bleed and die with you, ever since we got here."[9]

He saw love not as an emotion but as a process, and although he saw its tender side, he insisted that it be tough as well. "Love is a battle," he said. "Love is a war. Love is a growing up."[10]

Baldwin believed that gay bashing was as great an evil as racial persecution. Here, too, he believed that love was the answer. When he said

"Love all people," he meant *all* people—African Americans and whites, straights and gays.

It was the battle of James Baldwin's life, this battle for love. "I know that people can be better than they are," he wrote.[11] But he also knew that the opposite of love is hatred and that hatred can be just as powerful a force as love.

He saw that prejudice inspires the hatred which destroys love. Black people have long been the victims of this hatred. So have gays. But the greater damage, Baldwin believed, is to the souls of those who foster the hatred. And the greatest damage of all is to society at large— which is all of us.

Library and Church:
Books and Lessons

The father James Baldwin never knew was a key person in his life and in his writing. Like many children whose fathers are absent from their childhood, James thought about him a great deal. James asked his mother about him, but she only changed the subject. And so he imagined his father, he made things up, he painted a picture in his mind.

This picture was of a man sensitive, strong, and vulnerable. In James's imagination his father had stood up to the oppressive white world and had been destroyed by it. "He was reaching for the moon," James wrote, "[and] would therefore be dashed down against the rocks."[1]

But like other fatherless children, James resented his father's desertion and resented the man for not being there when he needed him. When James imagined his father in his first book, he had his father die before he was born. That way he could forgive his father's absence.

But James's father was not dead. James's mother, Emma Berdis Jones, knew who his father was, but she had been abandoned by him and she would never discuss him with anyone, let alone identify him to James. In fact, James's father seemingly wanted no part of him. They never met.

His mother was nineteen years old when she gave birth to James. She had come to New York City from Deal Island, Maryland, in the

South. She was one of many blacks who headed north in the 1920s, leaving behind a land of limited opportunity, legal segregation, and all too frequent lynchings by a newly active Ku Klux Klan. But she had no friends or family in New York, and for a young, pregnant, unmarried black woman the northern city was a harsh disappointment.

Harlem, the black area of New York City in which Emma settled, was looked at as the Promised Land by blacks all over the country. The early 1920s were the period known as the Harlem Renaissance, an explosion of black art and literature and poetry and music which had American whites focusing on black culture for the first time. But the pride blacks took in this cultural renaissance obscured the realities of life in Harlem, which included poverty, violence, degradation, and another—northern—kind of segregation.

View of an avenue in Harlem, 1927

Blacks beyond its borders viewed Harlem as a place where African Americans like band leader Duke Ellington and pianist Fats Waller were developing blues and jazz from a heritage of spirituals and African rhythms. They saw the Harlem that had given them the lyric poetry of Langston Hughes and the novels of Zora Neale Hurston. It was a Harlem of famous nightspots like the Cotton Club, a faraway, exciting place of bright lights and glitter. What they didn't see was the unemployment and disease and hunger, the despair which drove people to drink and drugs and prostitution.

This was the Harlem in which James Baldwin was raised. He was born there on August 2, 1924, at Harlem Hospital. Many years later, with a crooked grin and a certain proud defiance, he would say that he had been born "a kind of bastard."[2]

He was given the name Baldwin in 1927 when his mother married David Baldwin, a Baptist Pentecostal minister who also worked at a low-paying job in a bottling plant to make ends meet. The Reverend Baldwin was some forty years older than James's mother. He had been married before and had a daughter the same age as his new wife. Samuel, one of his children from his first marriage, lived with the Reverend, his new wife, and James. Samuel was eight years older than James.

The Reverend Baldwin's mother had been a slave. According to James, the Reverend himself had left the South because "lynching had become the national sport."[3] He was afraid of white people and acted respectfully toward them, but his hatred of all whites was bitter and deep. He did everything he could to make his children also hate them.

Despite the Reverend's advanced years, he fathered nine offspring during his marriage to James's mother. He was a stern man who believed in harsh discipline, and James, perhaps because he was not really his child, caught the full force of his fury. When James was very little, the Reverend whipped him with a belt for losing a dime. He never forgot the pain and humiliation of this early beating.

James was afraid of his stepfather, and he hated him. Yet at the same time he learned from him. Some of the lessons, though, were not the ones the Reverend had intended to teach him. His stepfather's casual brutality taught James that might is not always right. The

Reverend's blind fury toward all whites showed James how hatred of one race by another, no matter how justified it may seem, makes no sense in the end.

Some of the Reverend Baldwin's teachings James accepted at face value. James learned from his stepfather about preaching and the power of words and the might of God. He learned about the evils of drink and drugs and the dangers of casual sex. And he learned about responsibility and how a real man does not walk away from his problems or desert his children. These were standards James would value throughout his life.

Years later, when time had dulled James Baldwin's fear and hatred of his stepfather, he would remember "the pride and sorrow and beauty of my father's face: for that man I called my father really *was* my father in every sense except the biological, or literal one. He formed me, and he raised me, and he did not let me starve: and he gave me something, however harshly, and however little I wanted it, which prepared me for an impending horror which he could not prevent."[4]

The horror was that of growing up black among whites who were often, and sometimes without knowing it, oppressors of African Americans. Yet the first experiences James had with white people—a librarian, a schoolteacher—did not confirm this view.

While James was still in grade school, he had attracted the attention of a white teacher named Orilla Miller. She was impressed by his quick mind and willingness to learn and eagerness to read books. One day, after she'd known James awhile, she said she'd like to meet his parents.

The day James took Orilla Miller home his father wasn't there. It's possible that's why James chose that particular time for the visit. In any case, the visit made a deep impression on his teacher.

"That day," Orilla Miller wrote, "we stepped into a kitchen filled with steam because Mrs. Baldwin was doing the laundry by hand. There was a clothesline stretched the length of the room and there in the moist warmth were these many eager small children—his brothers and sisters. I was appalled at the poverty in which he lived."[5]

On another visit she did get to meet the Reverend Baldwin. Indeed, she came back many times when he was home. Sometimes she brought clothes for the children. James's stepfather grudgingly gave permission for Orilla Miller to take him to see Broadway plays. One, Shakespeare's *Macbeth*, impressed him deeply.

Despite Orilla Miller's kindnesses, the Reverend Baldwin was suspicious of her motives. In his eyes she was trying to make James smarter, and being too smart could be dangerous for a black boy. Down south he'd seen smart black boys whipped and even hanged. He made it plain that he didn't like this white woman, didn't want her around, and didn't want her charity. If he had known the number of plays and movies and museums to which she took James, he probably would have put a stop to the relationship.

James could not help but be influenced by his stepfather's sniping at Orilla Miller. He was a cautious boy and had seen enough to be wary of white people. But one day something happened to wash away that wariness, and he never doubted Orilla Miller again.

A downtown police station announced that they were handing out ice cream to children as a gesture of community goodwill. Orilla Miller rounded up James and some of his young brothers and sisters and took them to the station for a treat. The white police, used to the white children of the downtown neighborhood, were rattled. They had surely never intended to hand out free ice cream to *black* kids. They made it very clear that there was no ice cream forthcoming.

Writing about the incident later, James Baldwin couldn't recall anything Orilla Miller said to the police. "I just remember her face," he wrote, "as she stared at the cop, clearly intending to stand there until the ice cream all over the world melted or until the earth's surface froze, and she got us our ice cream, saying 'Thank you,' I remember, as we left."[6]

After that, James Baldwin could never hate *all* white people as his stepfather did.

As James entered his teens, he became more and more responsible for his younger halfbrothers and halfsisters. Samuel, the Reverend's son by his first marriage, whom James had looked up to as an older brother, had left home by now. James had regarded Samuel as a protector. He had loved him, and now he missed him very much. Still, he tried very hard to be to these new offspring what Samuel had been to him.

"My mother was given to the exasperating and mysterious habit of having babies," he remembered humorously in one of the essays in his second book, *Notes of a Native Son.* "As they were born, I took them over with one hand and held a book with the other."[7]

James approached books like "some kind of weird food" he could not stop eating.[8] He was addicted to them. He haunted the 135th Street branch of the New York Public Library. Here he discovered the Schomberg collection containing writings by African Americans and learned about the black experience and history from books like Booker T. Washington's *Up From Slavery.*

His love of reading had begun with two books which he read over and over again. One was *Uncle Tom's Cabin* by Harriet Beecher Stowe. Written in 1852 about the plight of black slaves in the South, it aroused the conscience of the nation against slavery.

Nine years after it was published, the United States was plunged into the Civil War. It is one of the handful of books ever written that may have changed history. Abraham Lincoln thought it had. When he first met Harriet Beecher Stowe, his greeting was "So you're the little woman who wrote the book that made this great war."[9]

Uncle Tom's Cabin taught James Baldwin, as it has taught millions of readers over the years, what life had been like for enslaved blacks on white-owned plantations. This was a part of his personal history, his "roots," and he valued it. But the novel taught him something else as well, a lesson that he would carry with him throughout his life as a writer: it taught him the power of words to change things for the better.

The other book he read and reread was *A Tale of Two Cities* by Charles Dickens. In Dickens he found portraits of wretched and starving poor white people in nineteenth-century France and England which struck him as very much like what he saw every day among the black people of Harlem. He learned from *A Tale of Two Cities* how being poor and hungry and oppressed can grind people down and make them bitter and cruel until one day they explode violently and strike down their oppressors. The influence of Dickens can be seen in Baldwin's most controversial work, *The Fire Next Time.*

Eventually, he read all of Dickens's books, beginning with those that were available at the 135th Street library. His aim was to read not just Dickens, but "all the books" in the branch, "an achievement that would, he felt, lend him the poise" to go into "the great main building of

UNCLE TOM'S CABIN;

OR,

LIFE AMONG THE LOWLY.

BY

HARRIET BEECHER STOWE.

VOL. I.

BOSTON:
JOHN P. JEWETT & COMPANY.
CLEVELAND, OHIO:
JEWETT, PROCTOR & WORTHINGTON.
1852.

FIRST EDITION, IN THE EXCESSIVELY RARE
RED CLOTH PRESENTATION BINDING

**Original title page for *Uncle Tom's Cabin*,
by Harriet Beecher Stowe**

James trembled when he saw the main reading room of the New York Public Library on 42nd Street and Fifth Avenue.

the Public Library," the Central Research Library guarded by stone lions on 42nd Street and Fifth Avenue.[10]

He regarded this building with awe and thought that "it must be full of corridors and marble steps, in the maze of which he would be lost and never find the book he wanted."[11] When Herman Porter, a white teacher at Frederick Douglass Junior High School, which James had entered in the fall of 1935, took him downtown to show him how to use the Research Library, James was so frightened that as they got off the bus he threw up on his teacher's shoes. In later years, as a writer, James would often use the Research Library.

James explained the effect books had on him as a child this way: "You think your pain and heartbreak are unprecedented in the history of the world, but then you read. It was books that taught me that the things that tormented me the most were the very things that connected me with all the people who were alive or who had ever been alive."[12]

Porter was not the only teacher who took an interest in James at Frederick Douglass Junior High. He also came under the influence of Countee Cullen, his French teacher. Cullen was already recognized as an important African-American poet. He was a graduate of New York University and had a master's degree from Harvard. He had founded the junior high school literary club. When he learned that James had won a prize for a short story which had appeared in a church newsletter, he persuaded him to join the club.

The young boy and the acclaimed poet had much in common. Both had been children of unwed mothers. Both had stepfathers who were stern ministers. Both felt themselves to be physically ugly.

James adored Cullen. He read all of his poetry that he could find. And he imitated his style when he began writing his own poetry in his teens. But sometimes James struggled for a different style, as in a poem from that time entitled "Black Girl Shouting." In part, it goes like this:

Black girl, whirl
Your torn, red dress.
Black girl, hide
Your bitterness.
Black girl, stretch
Your mouth so wide.
None will guess
The way he died.
Turned your heart
To quivering mud
While your lover's
Soft, red blood
Stained the scowling
Outraged tree.
Angels come
To cut him free! [13]

When he showed this poem to Countee Cullen, the teacher, usually so encouraging, told him, "It's an awful lot like Hughes."[14] Although he meant Langston Hughes, then recognized as the leading black poet in America, his tone made the words a put-down. Cullen and Hughes "were complete opposites in poetic style and approach" according to Hughes's biographer Faith Berry, and Cullen didn't really like Hughes's poetry.[15]

While Cullen may have dampened Baldwin's enthusiasm to write poetry, he always recognized his ability as a writer of prose and encouraged it. Cullen also urged James to apply for admission to DeWitt Clinton High School in the Bronx. At that time Clinton was among the top-rated schools in New York City. Clinton graduates include Richard Rodgers and Fats Waller, Charles Rangel and Neil Simon, Burt Lancaster and Nate Archibald, and many other high achievers. With Cullen's recommendation, James Baldwin was accepted at Clinton.

James was fourteen years old when he entered DeWitt Clinton. That was the same year that a school friend invited James to go to church with him. The church was Mount Calvary of the Pentecostal Faith Church. It was here he met a famous Harlem preacher, Mother Horn, who would one day be the model for the lead character in his play *The Amen Corner.*

The preaching of Mother Horn—Bishop Rosa Artemis Horn— stirred James to a religious pitch far beyond anything his stepfather had ever aroused. But there was trouble between her and her congregation, and James left Mount Calvary to join the Fireside Pentecostal Assembly. Here he became one of a group of young apprentice ministers. Soon he was the star of the group, and as news of his powerful speeches from the pulpit spread, James was called upon to preach at many Harlem churches.

He had a calling, a gift from God of the power to bring the spirit of the Lord to the flock. The Saints, as the most religious members of the Pentecostal congregations were known, responded to his sermons with joyous hallelujahs and amens that rocked the rafters. Even the Reverend Baldwin could not deny James's gift. And he could no longer pick on this stepson, who was now himself a minister in the "service of the Lord."[16]

Baldwin, shown here addressing students in the 1960s, developed his speaking skills as a young preacher in Harlem.

It was only natural that such success should go to James's head. His religious feelings were genuine, but this was also his first experience of the power of language to move people, and of his own power to use it to sway them. At the same time, Dewitt Clinton, located in the mostly white borough of the Bronx, was introducing him to a world of middle-class Italians and Jews who followed religions very different from his own.

At Clinton he had become friendly with two white boys, Emile Capouya, who would one day become a successful editor, and Richard Avedon, today a famous photographer. All three worked on the *Magpie*, the school's literary magazine. In his junior year at Clinton one of his teachers wrote that Baldwin "shows outstanding character in unselfish work as editor of the *Magpie*." Another praised his "modest, unassuming attitude in a class where he was an intellectual giant."[17]

But there is another side to Baldwin's record at Clinton. His first year there was something of a disaster. He had been an excellent student in junior high school, but he was no match for the high standards of Clinton. He failed geometry. He flunked Spanish. His average that first year was a low 63.

This was partly due to his concentration on writing sermons and performing his duties as an increasingly famous Harlem boy minister. The time he spent writing for and editing the *Magpie* and hanging out with his friends who worked on the magazine was also time taken away from his studies. The discussions James had with those he worked with on the *Magpie* brought the strict beliefs of his religion into question. These discussions troubled James. He knew that some questions can never be answered by logic and that this is where religion comes in and that it often requires a leap of faith. At the same time, the logic of his friends troubled him because they had made him question the faith pressed on him in childhood.

As James looked around at the churches of Harlem, it seemed that there were many hard preachers like his stepfather. And there were other preachers living high and riding around in fancy cars paid for by the hard-earned dollars their congregations put in the collection plate. He began to wonder about what he himself was doing, thinking of it as a magic show in which "I was behind the scenes and knew how the illusion was worked."[18]

James was tormented by religious doubts. Finally he discussed these doubts with his friend Emile Capouya. Emile suggested that James discuss them with an older man he knew, an artist named Beauford Delaney.

Delaney lived in Greenwich Village. He was a roly-poly African-American man in his thirties who had grown up with a minister father and understood the emotional grip of the church in Harlem. James and Delaney talked often about the conflict between James's desire to be a writer and his career as a minister. These talks showed Delaney that James had not really been exposed to much in art and music.

Delaney, himself a painter, thought it important to introduce James to the wonders of jazz and the blues. These were the African-American art forms that had influenced so many twentieth century composers in the United States and Europe. So he played the records of Louis Armstrong and Bessie Smith, Fats Waller and Ethel Waters and Ella Fitzgerald, Paul Robeson and Lena Horne. He answered the boy's eager questions about these black performers and their music. And in doing so he opened up a world that was rejected by the Pentecostal faith as filled with all sorts of sinful practices and evil places. But it was also a world for a writer.

More and more, James looked at the Church differently. "When we were told to love everybody, I had thought that meant *everybody*," he later wrote about his disillusionment. "But no. It applied only to those who believed as we did."[19]

The same year that he graduated from DeWitt Clinton High School, James, who had already stopped preaching, broke completely with the Church. He would later say that he "had to leave the church to save [my] soul."[20] But he could not totally reject it. "In spite of everything," he wrote, "there was in the life I fled a zest and a joy and a capacity for facing and surviving disaster that are very moving and very rare."[21]

This was the important lesson James took with him when he left the faith. In James Baldwin's life there would be insults and beatings, persecution for being black and for being gay. But James had learned that lesson.

"I am," he wrote, "a survivor."[22]

T H R E E

Goodbye to Harlem

At the end of 1941, the year James Baldwin graduated from high school, the United States was drawn into World War II. Harlem, like the rest of the country, was caught up in war fever. Work in defense plants opened up, relieving the joblessness of the Depression. Many young black men volunteered for the military; others were drafted.

Whether they were drafted or enlisted, they went into services that were segregated by color. Indeed, Harlem itself was segregated by the military. In many parts of the county, black soldiers on leave were forbidden to go into white districts, but in New York City Harlem was ruled off limits to white soldiers. Long before, with the end of the Harlem Renaissance and the deepening of poverty in Harlem, most white civilians had stopped coming there anyway. But the war and official segregation deepened the bitterness of Harlem.

James could not help feeling that bitterness. Why should a black man fight for a country and in an army that treated him as a second-class citizen? Street-corner speakers in Harlem asked the question, and the white police who dispersed the crowds they drew provided an answer of a sort. The answer was not lost on James.

He did not want to go to war and saw no reason why he should. Soon though, he would be old enough to be drafted. They might exempt him because he was the oldest of nine children in a family where his stepfather had recently become too sick to work. But a better course would be to get a job in a defense plant. Such jobs were often considered essential to the war effort. That, combined with his family status, would surely keep him out of the service. Besides, the family badly needed the money James could earn.

His white friend Emile Capouya found a job in a defense plant in New Jersey and moved there. A while later he helped James get a job in the same factory. James moved in with Emile.

James soon found out that New Jersey wasn't Harlem. Nor was it Greenwich Village, where he'd been spending so much time with Beauford Delaney. New Jersey in the early 1940s was a northern white state with lots of southern prejudices.

The wartime factories had drawn poor Southerners, white and black, to Jersey for jobs. The black Southerners behaved as they always had toward white Southerners—with fear and respect. For the most part, the white Southerners treated all African Americans the same—with arrogance and contempt.

James, however, didn't behave like most of the other blacks at work. He acted as he had always acted—with pride. His white co-workers saw him as "uppity." They insulted him and they threatened him. James complained to the managers of the factory. Instead of acting on his complaint they fired him. He quickly found another job at a nearby plant, but the situation was the same. The white Southerners here also persecuted the blacks. James truly believed that if he gave them an excuse, they would stomp him into the ground, perhaps even kill him.

This daily persecution resulted in "a kind of blind fever, a pounding in the skull and fire in the bowels," Baldwin remembered in *Notes of a Native Son*.[1] He added, "There is not a Negro alive who does not have this rage in his blood."[2]

One night James went to a restaurant that catered to college boys. "Negroes were not served there, I was told," Baldwin recalled. "I determined to go there all the time. But now they were ready for me and though some dreadful scenes were subsequently enacted in that restaurant, I never ate there."[3]

He found the same racial prejudice in New Jersey's "bars, bowling alleys, diners, places to live." But he didn't take it lying down. He began to get a reputation for making scenes. "Children giggled behind me when I passed and their elders whispered or shouted—they really believed that I was mad."[4]

One night James and a white friend went to a movie in Trenton, the capital of New Jersey. After the show they went to a diner which refused to serve James. "I felt . . . a *click* at the nape of my neck," he later recalled. He went to a second diner where the waitress told him, "We don't serve Negroes here." James picked up a water jug and flung it, shattering the mirror behind the counter. "I rose and began running for the door." A man grabbed him and began beating him. A crowd began to gather, a white crowd. He ran from it as fast as he was able. "I could have been murdered," he realized later. But what was even more shocking to him was that "I had been ready to commit murder."[5]

Back in Harlem, things had gone from bad to worse for the Baldwin family with James gone. His mother was pregnant with her ninth child by the Reverend Baldwin, her tenth altogether, counting James. Although there were jobs available for black men now, James's stepfather, at almost eighty years of age, was too old to lay claim to any of them. In idleness the Reverend's frequent rages had begun to alternate with periods of deep depression. He accused his wife, and sometimes his children, of trying to poison him. Finally he had to be put in the mental ward of a hospital.

Here it was discovered that the Reverend Baldwin had for some time had tuberculosis. It was too far gone to do anything about. There was no doubt that his mental state had to some degree been caused by the disease.

On July 29, 1943, the Reverend David Baldwin died. A few hours later his wife gave birth to a baby girl, Paula. The funeral was held on August 2, James's nineteenth birthday, and the burial was slated for the next day.

About a month before the Reverend's death a violent race riot had broken out in Detroit, Michigan. Harlem had watched and waited. It was still waiting when James came home from New Jersey. "I had never known it to be so violently still," James wrote. "I had never before been so aware of policemen, on foot, on horseback, on corners, everywhere."[6]

The night of the Reverend Baldwin's funeral — the night before the burial — Harlem exploded. The spark that set off the explosion was the rumor that a black soldier on leave in Harlem had been shot in the back by a white policeman in the Hotel Braddock while defending a black woman being hassled by the officer. The rumor was that the soldier was dead.

In fact, the woman was a prostitute whom the officer was trying to move out of the hotel lobby. In fact, the black soldier had not been shot in the back. In fact, he was not dead.

But in the wartime climate of Harlem the truth didn't matter. There were riots. The National Guard was called out. Mobs fought the police

**Witnessing scenes like this one, Baldwin noted:
"Harlem had needed something to smash."**

and the guardsmen and stampeded through the streets torching and looting stores. Many people were arrested. There were countless injuries. Five African Americans really were shot and killed.

The day after the first night of rioting, the hearse containing the remains of the Reverend Baldwin moved through Harlem on the way to the cemetery. James was in a car in the funeral procession which followed. He noted the devastation, the burned-out stores, the broken plate-glass windows, the scraps of torn clothing, and the occasional dried pools of blood. "Harlem," he later wrote—not condoning the destruction, but understanding it all too well—"had needed something to smash."[7]

But James was trapped in Harlem. After his stepfather's death and the birth of the new baby, he had to return home to help out. He worked at a series of meaningless jobs—in a meatpacking plant, in clothing factories in the garment district, as a dishwasher, running an elevator. He was drifting and he was unhappy, and at the end of the working day there was always Harlem waiting, the overcrowded apartment, the screaming kids.

Sometimes, unable to face it, he went down to Greenwich Village and spent time with Beauford Delaney. The older man understood what James was going through. He too had lived in Harlem. He urged James to leave there. Above all he urged him to continue with his writing.

James tried. He'd push himself into a corner of his family's crowded apartment with a pad on his knees and try to write. He'd try to shut out the noise and confusion around him. He'd write a few lines, perhaps a page, and then he would be forced to give it up. A writer needs privacy; it was the one thing he could never have in Harlem living with his mother and her nine other children.

Some nights James just stayed downtown after work. He wandered the mean streets of Times Square, a sleazy area even back then. He went to the all-night movies on 42nd Street and dozed through them. Much later this time in his life would provide the opening for James's novel *Another Country:*

> He was facing Seventh Avenue, at Times Square. It was past
> midnight and he had been sitting in the movies, in the top

row of the balcony, since two o'clock in the afternoon. . . .
He was so tired, he had fallen so low. . . . He was hungry,
his mouth felt filthy. . . . And he was broke. And he had
nowhere to go. The policeman passed him, giving him
a look.[8]

He would remember it as the most hopeless period in his life, and
James would do with it what a writer must do with his worst times: he
would write about it. But back then it seemed more and more that writing was beyond him. Unable to write at home, he would go into one of
the all-night cafeterias around Times Square and sit at a table and try to
write there. He would write a little and then feel guilty about not having
gone home and be unable to write more.

When James did go home, the guilt turned to anger. He was sarcastic to his mother. He treated his sisters badly. He yelled at his brothers.
His love for his family was turning to resentment and hate. He didn't
want to be there in Harlem with them. He wanted to be free of them.
He wanted to write. One day he looked in the mirror and saw in his
face the fury which was his sharpest memory of his stepfather's face.
And he was frightened.

He poured out his fear to Beauford Delaney. The artist helped him
see that if he stayed at home his resentment toward his family would increase. He would become bitter and his bitterness would hurt his family
more than help them. Finally James was convinced. He left Harlem
and moved into Delaney's Greenwich Village apartment.

James found in the Village a freedom different from any he had
known in Harlem, or in Jersey. In those days there was plenty of prejudice, even in the Village, against blacks and homosexuals. Over the
years James would encounter his share of this bigotry. But it was not
part of the Village scene that Delaney introduced to James.

The circles Delaney moved in included painters and writers, jazz
musicians and skat singers, dancers and sculptors, out-of-work actors
and merchant seamen between ships, radicals and dropouts. It was a
live-and-let-live group in which blacks and Latinos and whites and
Christians and Jews and straights and gays talked and argued and
sometimes screamed at each other, but did not hate. Ideas were the

currency they spent freely on one another. James took to this scene like a duck to water.

He got a job waiting tables at the Calypso, a small restaurant run by a kindhearted West Indian woman who gave him food to pass along to his brothers and sisters when they came downtown to visit him. Many celebrities and celebrities-to-be, black and white, came into the Calypso. Among them were Malcolm X, Delaney's friend Henry Miller, Paul Robeson, Burt Lancaster, Eartha Kitt, and Marlon Brando, who would become James's lifelong friend.

James really liked the job. For the most part the customers treated him not as a waiter but as an equal. They would draw him into their arguments. Ideas whirled around him as he balanced his tray and sometimes he would shout out his opinions over the noise as he moved from table to table.

In the Village it was possible to feel comfortable with his sexuality. His new freedom unloosed his creativity. He returned to his writing with added energy. Soon he had written fifty pages of the book that would become his first published novel, *Go Tell It on the Mountain.* And then a miracle happened. A friend who had read James's work knew Richard Wright and arranged for James to call on him.

Richard Wright was the most acclaimed African-American novelist of the 1940s. His work raised the question that had been ignored by whites since the end of the Civil War: "How may a black man live in a country which denies his humanity?"[9] His novel *Native Son* was a wake-up call for white America. In it a young black man named Bigger Thomas accidentally kills a white woman. When the white world comes to punish him, he fights back. Bigger's rage is the rage many black people feel toward whites because of their treatment by them. For the first time this rage stood naked on the printed page.

James Baldwin had of course read the book. But it was Orson Welles's stage version of *Native Son* that left the impression he would never forget. It starred Canada Lee, the powerful black boxer turned actor, as Bigger Thomas. "I will not forget Canada Lee's performance as long as I live," wrote Baldwin.[10] "His physical presence gave me the right to live."[11] Now, on his way to visit Richard Wright, James pic-

**Richard Wright gave Baldwin his
first break in the publishing world.**

tured him as looking like Canada Lee, as having the fire of Bigger
Thomas.

But Wright "was not like that at all," James would remember. "His
voice was light and even rather sweet, . . . his body was more round
than square, more square than tall; and his grin was more boyish than I
had expected."[12] He greeted James, who had come to his house in
Brooklyn hoping to show him his writing, with a "Hey Boy!" and the
offer of a glass of bourbon. James "was terrified that the liquor, on my
empty stomach" would make him sick.[13]

They discussed writing while James sipped carefully at his drink. Wright paid attention to what James had to say. Then, casually, he asked if he might see some of James's writing. His heart beating wildly, James agreed to send him the finished pages of *Go Tell It on the Mountain.*

Wright read the manuscript and liked it very much. He recommended James for a Eugene F. Saxton Foundation Fellowship, which included a grant of $500, no small amount in those days. In November 1945, at age twenty-one, James received the grant and was taken to lunch by Wright's publisher at Harper & Brothers.

James was a very young man when he received the grant. It was the first major recognition of his work, and it came from a famous writer and publisher as well as from the foundation which gave him the money. It was a great honor for one so young, but it also placed a responsibility on him to finish his novel.

He wasn't ready for the responsibility. He was young and inexperienced. He felt unsure of his talent, and now there was this pressure to prove himself. It turned the writing of his novel sour and then blocked it altogether.

When he forced himself to write the results weren't good. Harper & Brothers, the first publisher to show serious interest in his writing, now rejected his work. James felt that he had let down Richard Wright, who had sponsored him at Harper. Feeling miserable and depressed, he stopped work on the novel.

James was depressed after the rejection by Harper. It was a condition he shared with a friend named Eugene Worth. It led to their drinking too much and too often and getting drunk and sometimes behaving badly. They called their condition "desolate demoralization."[14] Eugene, however, was much more desolate and much more demoralized than James. In December 1946 Eugene Worth, age 24, killed himself.

It was both a terrible shock and a terrible loss to James. It would be many years before he could deal with it. When he did, it would be through the character of Rufus, the African-American hero who dominates the first section of his novel *Another Country.* Many critics, including some who did not like the book as a whole, consider this section Baldwin's most powerful fiction writing.

In *Another Country* Rufus's death is patterned after Eugene's real-life suicide. Like Eugene, Rufus kills himself by jumping off what Baldwin ironically describes as "the bridge built to honor the father of his country"[15]—the George Washington Bridge—which connects upper Manhattan and New Jersey. James Baldwin envisions his friend's death:

> Then he stood on the bridge, looking over, looking down. . . .
> There were muted lights on the Jersey shore and here and
> there a neon flame advertising something somebody had
> for sale. He began to walk slowly to the center of the
> bridge, observing that from this height, the city which had
> been so dark as he walked through it seemed to be on fire.
> He stood at the center of the bridge and it was freezing
> cold. . . . He began to cry. . . . He knew the pain would
> never stop. He could never go down into the city again. . . .
> It was cold and the water would be cold. He was black and
> the water was black. . . . He felt a shoe fly off behind him,
> there was nothing around him, only the wind.[16]

James was tormented by Eugene Worth's death. But he also saw in Eugene's destruction the possibility of his own. Painful as the suicide was, it was also a warning to James. He eased off on his drinking and running around. He began to take himself and his life more seriously.

He started to write again. He didn't go back to the novel. He wasn't ready for that. But through various friends he did manage to get assignments for book reviews.

James Baldwin's first piece in a recognized publication appeared in the *Nation* on April 12, 1947, four months after Eugene's death. It was a review of a book by the Russian novelist Maxim Gorki, which James found overly sentimental. This was followed by a review of a biography of Frederick Douglass which he said did nothing for "interracial understanding."[17] This one is memorable for containing a sentence that typifies how James felt about race relations, even as a young man. "Relations between Negroes and whites," the 22-year-old Baldwin wrote, "must be based on the assumption that there is one race and we are all part of it."[18] He meant, of course, the human race.

Young as he was, during the following year James built a reputation as a talented reviewer. Then, in April 1948 his review in the *New Leader* of a new historical romance saga called *Raintree County* by a young author named Ross Lockridge caused a furor. He had panned the novel as "superficial" and poked fun at its sugarcoated vision of America.[19]

When Lockridge committed suicide before the review was published, James was asked to add a postscript to soften his harsh criticism. But what he wrote only further mocked the dead author's work, comparing it to "Sunday School and Boy Scout Meetings."[20] Some readers were shocked at Baldwin's insensitivity; others admired him for sticking to his guns.

Also in 1948, *Commentary* published James's first full-length essay. Entitled "The Harlem Ghetto," it was on anti-Semitism in Harlem. It turned a spotlight on black urban attitudes and the reasons for them, which many Jewish and African-American leaders would have been just as happy to ignore. Written over forty years before the terrible riots in Brooklyn's Crown Heights, which pitted blacks against Jews, the essay reads like prophecy.

"Both the Negro and the Jew are helpless," wrote Baldwin, pointing out that "the pressure of living" leaves no "time for understanding." He concluded that "just as a society must have a scapegoat, so hatred must have a symbol. Georgia has the Negro and Harlem has the Jew."[21]

Baldwin's main point was that blacks were prejudiced against Jews first and foremost because they were white, not because they were Jewish. This prejudice was the mirror image of white prejudice toward blacks. He believed that the prejudice of some Jews toward blacks was a result of their becoming part of an American society where such prejudice has been part of the national tradition since slavery.

There was probably less prejudice against African Americans in the Village than in any other part of the United States, but it was far from being free of prejudice. This is reflected in his first published short story, which appeared in the October 1948 issue of *Commentary*. It concerned a problem James knew firsthand—the indignities a black man faces renting a room from a white landlord in Greenwich Village.

In his story, titled "Previous Condition," the young black man is sneaked into a room rented by his Jewish friend. When the landlady finds him, she tells him "I can't have no colored people here."[22] He flees to Harlem, but he doesn't feel at home there as he does in the liberated atmosphere of the Village.

This was a reflection of how James himself felt about Harlem. Yet the Village's acceptance of blacks, as the story demonstrates, was limited. The attitude of the country as a whole toward blacks, as he had defined it in "The Harlem Ghetto," dictated the Village bigotry. It was the United States—the country—which did not accept him. It was the nation which James increasingly felt he must escape.

He would never be able to get back to his novel and finish it in this country. He had to get out, to get away. But how?

FOUR

Paris

Often in James Baldwin's life, luck would step in and make it possible for him to do what he most wanted to do. In 1948 what he most wanted to do was to get out of the United States. He wanted to go to Paris. To a young writer it was *the* place to go, the city where writers went to write.

At this time he and a photographer friend, Theodore Pelatowski, wanted to do a book with pictures and text on the storefront churches of Harlem. They submitted samples of the book to every publisher they knew and all rejected it. But then, on the basis of a three-page proposal, they won a grant from the Julian Rosenwald Foundation.

James's share of the money was $1,500. He gave a little more than half of it to his mother, keeping $700 for himself—enough to buy an airplane ticket to Paris. The ticket cost $660. He arrived in Paris with $40 in his pocket.

His first view of Paris as the plane descended filled him with "the absolute certainty of being dashed to death on the vindictive tooth of the Eiffel Tower."[1] Once on the ground, however, he fell in love with the city. After the storefront churches of Harlem, he was dazzled by the ancient cathedrals—Notre Dame with its expressive gargoyles; Sacre Coeur's breathtaking view of the Paris rooftops. The broad boulevards, the arched bridges, the magnificent gardens, the Louvre, the Arch of Triumph, the opera house, the Grand Palace—the beauty of Paris enchanted James.

The days filled his eyes and at night he found himself "singing, loving every inch of France," his ears exploding with "the jam sessions at Pigalle." He stayed up until daybreak with new friends, "telling stories, sad and earnest stories, in grey workingmen's cafes."[2]

Summing up his feelings for the city, James wrote, "Every Negro in America carries all through his life the burden of race consciousness like a corpse on his back. I shed that corpse when I stepped off the train in Paris."[3]

James moved into the Hotel Verneuil on the Left Bank of the Seine River, which divides the city. This was the area where artists and writers congregated. It was also, in the aftermath of World War II, an area filled with the sounds of American jazz. Many black musicians had come there from the United States and found an eager reception for their music and a relatively prejudice-free reception for themselves.

Mostly though, in his early days in Paris, James hung out with American writers, and most of them were white. They included Philip Roth and Saul Bellow and Truman Capote. Capote's advice to James about writing was to "go back where we all come from . . . and do it there or you are in danger of losing your perspective."[4] Although James ignored the advice at the time, he would comment later that he had never felt so much an American as when he had been in France awhile. If blacks were treated badly in the United States, it was nevertheless James's home and always would be. In Paris he would always be an American.

Richard Wright was in Paris and introduced James to the French philosopher-writer Jean-Paul Sartre, as well as to the publishers of *Zero*, a new magazine. Wright praised James's work as a book reviewer and essayist back in New York. As a result, the publishers asked James to write for *Zero*.

His first piece for the magazine was an essay called "Everybody's Protest Novel." It criticized Wright's best-known work, *Native Son*. James compared Bigger Thomas, the novel's hero, to Harriet Beecher Stowe's

**Truman Capote, an American
writer Baldwin met in Paris**

overly humble Uncle Tom, saying that "Bigger is Uncle Tom's descendant, flesh of his flesh."[5] According to Baldwin's biographer Lisa Rosset, "The article deeply hurt the older writer and soured their friendship."[6]

James also wrote an article called "The Negro in Paris" for the *Reporter.* In it he confessed that he could not relate easily to black Africans in Paris. They only seemed to confirm his feelings that he was himself "peculiarly American."[7]

These Africans were mostly students from various countries and black Algerian workers. James had gone out of his way to seek them out in the bistros where they gathered. But he could not identify with them. The African history and experience was too different from that of the African American's. While it was true that their countries had been seized as colonies by white European nations, their ancestors had not been an oppressed minority as James's ancestors had. They may have lived in nations stripped of their wealth, but they were black nations. They did not live in a white-dominated land. Contact with them left James as it had found him—a victim and critic of America who was nevertheless himself an American.

One result of James's contact with the Algerians was that he got a job as a singer in an Arab cafe. One night he had showed up there after having had too much to drink and had belted out the song "Lover Man" for some Algerian acquaintances. The owner of the place liked his voice and hired him. But the job didn't last long; in his bones James was a writer, not a singer.

French philosopher Jean-Paul Sartre

He had taken the job because he couldn't pay his rent from the money he earned for the occasional pieces he wrote. He could have written more for magazines and journals, but he had set aside time to work on his novel. He was rewriting steadily and was determined to finish it and find a publisher. But James was always broke.

"He could never afford to buy cigarettes or drinks," remembers a friend from those Paris days. "He would borrow and then, of course, be unable to pay back."[8]

Although James's friends remembered him as "laughing all the time," events would show that this was a cover-up for a deepening unhappiness that was causing him to drink too much.[9] The drinking interfered with his work and this, of course, made him more unhappy.

The drinking contributed to his becoming run-down. He sometimes fell ill and was forced to take to his bed. Twice, severely swollen glands caused him to be hospitalized.

Even shorter of money than usual because of his illness, James was forced to take a room in the Grand Hotel du Bac. As hotels go, it was run-down and dismal and anything but grand.

It was definitely not the sort of place where James wanted to spend a lot of time in his room. To get away from it, he would go to one or another of the sidewalk cafes in the area. The idea was to have a drink, sit at a table, and get some writing done. Some nights though, with the novel not going well and feeling more and more depressed, James would do more drinking than writing.

On one of those nights he was spotted by a tourist who had known him back in New York. When the man sat down and began complaining bitterly about his hotel, James offered to get him a room at the Grand Hotel du Bac.

The man was so furious at the hotel he had moved out of that when he left he took "a bedsheet belonging to his hotel and put it in his suitcase." As James later described the incident, "when he arrived at my hotel, I borrowed the sheet, since my own were filthy and the chambermaid showed no sign of bringing me any clean ones, and put it on my bed."[10]

One evening two French detectives showed up looking for the stolen sheet. They found it on James's bed. He was arrested.

"But is this very serious?" James asked them.[11]

"It's not serious," was the answer. "It's nothing at all."[12] At the police station, James was placed in a small cell. He had heard the French word for *American* used and it dawned on him that while they might have nothing against him for being black, their tone said they had little use for citizens of the United States. The fact that he spent the night in the cell with no further contact with the police seemed to confirm this.

James had been arrested on December 19, 1949. His trial was set for December 24, the day before Christmas. Meanwhile, he continued to be held in prison. However, because of the holiday, the interpreter was not available that day. James spent Christmas Eve and Christmas Day in prison.

On December 27, finally, he went to trial. The case was dismissed, but not before the story of the stolen bedsheet had been told and aroused what Baldwin would describe as "great merriment in the courtroom."[13] The laughter had a dreadful effect on Baldwin. He heard it as "the laughter I had often heard at home" and he interpreted it as "the laughter of those who consider themselves to be at a safe remove from all the wretched, for whom the pain of living is not real."[14]

More than anything else, it was that laughter which left him horribly depressed. Then, when he got back to his hotel, he was met by his landlady demanding the rent he owed her. She threatened to evict him if he didn't pay immediately. Of course he had no money and couldn't pay.

It was too much for James. The world was too cruel. He went up to his room, took a sheet off the bed, tied one end around a ceiling pipe, climbed up on a chair, and tied the other end around his neck. Then he kicked the chair out from under him.

The pipe to which he had tied the sheet broke. It was a water pipe. James fell to the floor, water pouring from the ceiling and drenching him.

He exploded with laughter. He was overwhelmed by it. What a world! What a life!

James saw it clearly then—briefly, but clearly. Life is a comedy. Life is a tragedy. And sometimes the two are the same.

FIVE

Lucien and "Giovanni's Room"

The suicide attempt with its slapstick ending somehow renewed James's appetite for living. He was unable to stop smiling at the memory of the burst water pipe, and things no longer seemed so bad to him. After all, there was the bustle of Paris all around him, a book to be written, new people to meet and get to know.

Lucien Happersberger was one. He was a 17-year-old from Switzerland, and he would be the inspiration for James's second novel, *Giovanni's Room*. It would tell the story of a love affair between two men, one an uptight white American, the other—Giovanni—a spontaneous Italian.

"I met Giovanni," the American narrator of Baldwin's novel would remember, "during my second year in Paris, when I had no money. On the morning of the evening that we met I had been turned out of my room."[1]

Lucien was a well-tanned white youth, muscular, a little tough-looking, but with a sensitive face and deep, dark eyes. Although eight years younger than Baldwin, he was every bit as streetwise. He had run away to Paris from his middle-class home in Switzerland. When James met him he had been in Paris for a while, living by his wits.

Lucien and "Giovanni's Room"

"I think we connected the instant that we met," the narrator of *Giovanni's Room* would remember.[2] Certainly it was that way with James and Lucien. It was the beginning of the relationship James would describe as the "love of my life."[3] Lucien saw it differently. "We were buddies," he would remember. Still, he couldn't deny that "Jimmy was very romantic. He had a dream of settling down."[4] Lucien didn't share the dream.

After that first meeting, James and Lucien saw each other constantly over the next two years. They didn't live together, but they were always in each other's company at mealtimes and at cafes. Also, they took trips together.

Being broke all the time was a problem for both of them. It was more expensive to live in Paris than in most other places in Europe, particularly rural areas. The constant worrying about money was interfering with James's writing. The excitement of Paris, which he adored, also distracted him. He felt himself very close to finishing *Go Tell It on the Mountain,* but he needed to get away to someplace quiet and peaceful and without the daily pressures of the city.

Lucien contrived a solution. Through a friend in a laboratory he got hold of a set of X rays of lungs which were beginning to develop tuberculosis. He brought these X rays to his father and passed them off as his own. The doctors, he told his father, said that he must spend a number of months in the cool, clear air of the Swiss mountains.

His father had a chalet—a small vacation home—in Loeche-les-Bains. This remote Alpine village was known for the health-restoring waters of its underground springs. Persuaded that his son's health was at stake, Lucien's father agreed to let him and a friend use the chalet. He would send Lucien fifty Swiss francs a month to see him through his illness. Lucien and James went to Loeche-les-Bains during the autumn of 1951.

The day James arrived, he heard "the children shout *Neger! Neger!*" he recalled later. He "was far too shocked to have any real reaction."[5] There were only a few hundred people in Loeche-les-Bains, and they had never seen a nonwhite person before. They tried to touch his skin and his tightly curled hair. He understood that there was no malice in their reaction to him. *Nee-ger* did not mean to them what *nigger* might mean to an American bigot. Nevertheless, it hurt.

When he came to Loeche-les-Bains, James had been working on his first novel for eight long years. Now, despite the reaction to his skin color, he found the peace of mind to finish it. On February 26, 1952, he mailed it off to a literary agent in New York.

It was done. He had told his story. *Go Tell It on the Mountain* was a novel, but it was very much James's story. In its pages, he had faced his stepfather and wrestled him to the ground and not beaten him, but rather come to understand him. He had seen past the brutality and the harshness and found the love he had never been shown. James Baldwin would write other books, but he would never again know so personal a triumph through his writing.

The book was sent by James's agent to the publisher Alfred Knopf, who liked it but wanted to discuss revisions before agreeing to publish it. James had to go to New York. But first he returned to Paris to try to scrounge up enough money to pay for the trip.

He was in luck. In Paris he ran into his old friend Marlon Brando, whose movie career was beginning to skyrocket. Brando loaned him the money for the trip home.

In New York the revisions went well and Knopf agreed to publish *Mountain.* James received a $1,000 advance against royalties for the novel. The book would never go out of print between then and now, and James would earn many times the amount of the advance from its sales.

His visit home lasted only a few months, but it put him back in touch with what it meant to be an African American. While he was living in Europe, the segregation imposed so erratically on blacks in America had faded from his mind. His younger brother Wilmer, however, had joined the recently desegregated Army and was facing it there. He wrote home bitterly about constant harassment from a white officer who didn't like blacks. And then it went beyond harassment. "One of my brothers, in uniform, had his front teeth kicked out by a white officer," James would recall in *Nobody Knows My Name.*[6]

When his brother's bitterness turned to feelings of worthlessness and thoughts of suicide, James wrote to him. He pointed out that fear and guilt were the roots of racism. James cautioned his brother against falling into the trap of hatred, which was the same trap as that in which the white bigot is caught. These were beliefs that he would express in a variety of ways in the essays he wrote over the years. They would lead him to the conviction that conquering prejudice was only possible by overcoming hatred with love.

This was not a view that he embraced blindly, or by ignoring his feelings. It wasn't pleasant to be reminded of what black people were subjected to in his native land, and James would never excuse or forgive it. White Americans had a lot to answer for—either because of what they had done to black people, or because of things they hadn't done to end black people's oppression.

But he wasn't ready to come to grips with American racism at this time. There was an idea for a new novel he was eager to begin writing. He also wanted to gather his magazine essays into a book, hoping that if *Mountain* was successful they could be published. And he missed Lucien very much. He used part of his book advance to pay for passage back to Europe.

When he got to Loeche-les-Bains, Lucien had some stunning news for him. He had become deeply involved with a young woman named Suzy, and now she was expecting his baby. "What should I do?" he asked.[7]

James was deeply hurt, but he didn't hesitate to answer. He knew all too well the pain of being the child of an unwed mother. He felt very strongly the obligation of the father in such a case. "Marry her," he told Lucien.[8]

He had given up the "love of my life" because he believed one must do the right thing.[9] And so Lucien and Suzy were married. The child was born in October and James was its godfather. The proud parents named it Luc James after Lucien and Baldwin.

Seven months later, in May 1953, *Go Tell It on the Mountain* was published. The reviews were very positive. It was called everything from beautiful to fierce to brutal to objective. James was compared to such great writers as James Joyce and William James, Richard Wright and William Faulkner. He was praised for his "insight and authoritative realism" and recognized as a talented young novelist with a bright career in front of him.[10]

But he was still broke.

Those first days back in Paris after the publication of *Go Tell It on the Mountain* were particularly hard for James. As the summer of 1953 turned into autumn, according to his biographer David Leeming, "he felt trapped by poverty and was unable to write."[11]

His picture was taken for *Time* magazine, but when he went to a celebrity gathering, it was in a borrowed suit. He could not afford to get the one suit he owned out of the cleaners. He became more and more depressed. But then one day, sitting at a table at a sidewalk cafe, he looked up and saw Beauford Delaney.

The artist had come to Paris to paint. James could not have been more delighted to see him. The older man had been like a father to him in New York. Delaney had lent him money, given him a roof over his head, and encouraged him to stick with his writing. If he hadn't had Delaney's support as a youth, he might never have written *Go Tell It on the Mountain.*

Delaney asked him what he was working on, and James had to admit that he wasn't really working at all. The next question was what would James be working on if he was working? James told his friend about his notes for *Giovanni's Room,* as well as an idea he'd been kicking around for a book of essays and the play he intended to write. That was a lot of work not to be working on, and he and Delaney laughed about that.

They saw a lot of each other. Always Delaney pushed James to get back to his writing. But instead James sat with Delaney at sidewalk cafes and drank wine. Delaney really did value James as a writer as well as a friend. He could see that James was sliding farther and farther away from his work. The older man urged James to get out of Paris, to go someplace quiet and without distractions, someplace where he would be able to spend his time writing instead of drinking.

Finally James took his advice. He said good-bye to Delaney, left Paris, and went to the south of France. He settled in Les Quatre Chemins, a small, peaceful village with no nightlife. Here he limited his drinking and set to work in earnest on his writing.

The village was very isolated, and so was James. He was out of touch with what was happening back in the United States. The 1954 Supreme Court decision ending segregation in public schools went unnoticed by him.

Laws in the South had long held that black children and white children could not go to the same schools. They were to be educated in schools that were "separate but equal." Now Chief Justice Earl Warren, speaking for the Court, ruled that "in the field of public education, the doctrine of separate but equal has no place" because separated schools "are inherently unequal."[12]

The schools were directed to integrate. Many white Southerners and their leaders vowed never to seat black and white children in the same classrooms. They would not obey the Court's order; they would defy the law.

Lines had been drawn for a battle over civil rights which would escalate and go on for many years. One day James Baldwin would be a part of that battle and a major spokesman for those who fought for civil rights. But now he was finishing work on his play.

James called the play *The Amen Corner.* It was set in a storefront church in Harlem. The main character, Sister Margaret, was based on Mother Horn, the dynamic Pentecostal minister who had inspired James to become a boy preacher. When the play was finished, he decided to go to New York to see about having it produced.

The *Amen Corner* excited little interest in New York. One Broadway producer after another declined to produce it. Indeed, although there would be an earlier amateur production which would focus attention on the play, it would be twelve years before *The Amen Corner* would be produced on Broadway. And Knopf, which had brought out *Go Tell It on the Mountain,* refused to publish the play.

James was very disappointed. Rage and bitterness overwhelmed the disappointment one night when he had a run-in with the police. He and an acquaintance named Themistocles Hoetis were walking toward a subway station when they found themselves in the center of a melee involving a bunch of youths who had stolen a lamp from a nearby bar. "The whole lot of us were surrounded by cops and we were all arrested," recalls Hoetis.[13]

The unfairness and the indignity were too much for James. "They put him in a cell next to me," according to Hoetis, "and he just screamed all night long: *I'm a nigger!* They picked me up because I'm black!'"[14]

After spending the night in jail, James was brought to court the next morning. He was charged with disorderly conduct. He had, the police said, resisted an order to move along. The judge found him guilty but gave him a suspended sentence. James was a free man, but his fury at the racism of his native land had been refueled.

His anger over the incident smoldered for a long time, and he got little work done. But eventually he retreated to a writers colony in Saratoga Springs, New York, and began writing again. He worked steadily on *Giovanni's Room* and on revising the essays, largely dealing with race, which he had published in magazines between 1948 and 1955. This was the collection that would be published later that year as *Notes of a Native Son.*

The writing was interrupted temporarily by an offer from the Howard University Players to put on *The Amen Corner.* While they were only an amateur college group, they had an excellent reputation and professionals in the theater followed their productions closely. Howard, once an all-black university, had begun attracting white students after World War II. However, it was still considered one of the leading black colleges in the country and there was a conflict among some African-American faculty members over Baldwin's play.

His use of what would become known as Black English was at the center of the argument. The dialogue was written the way the people of Harlem actually spoke. "This play will set back the Speech Department thirty years," one teacher complained.[15]

But the movement was already beginning among black scholars to view the speech patterns of poor blacks—a mixture of southern dialect and inner-city street slang—as a legitimate and poetic expression of their feelings and their lifestyles. *The Amen Corner* was one of the earliest examples of a work in Black English. Others would follow and gain acceptance among whites as well as blacks. James himself thought Black English more lyrical and vivid than standard English. Today it is a recognized—if still controversial—form of expression.

Not long after the Howard production of *The Amen Corner,* Beacon Press published *Notes of a Native Son.* Its essays established James, who had just celebrated his thirty-first birthday, as a spokesperson for

American blacks. "The world is white no longer," he reminded the nation at the end of the final essay, "and it will never be white again."[16]

Generally, his message was one of tolerance and integration between blacks and whites. It was critical of white people, but it did not reject them. Some African Americans thought he let whites off much too easily.

Langston Hughes was one. The most famous African-American poet reviewed *Notes* in *The New York Times*. "Baldwin's viewpoints are half American, half Afro-American, incompletely fused," Hughes wrote. James was hurt by the criticism.[17]

By that time he had been back in France for four months putting the finishing touches to *Giovanni's Room*. He dedicated the book to Lucien and sent it off to New York to Knopf. However, since homosexuality was still illegal just about everywhere in the United States, the publisher was afraid of legal action and refused to bring out *Giovanni's Room*. Other major publishers also rejected it.

Then, in the spring of 1956, James's luck changed. He received a $1,000 grant from the National Institute of Arts and Letters. It was followed by a $3,000 fellowship from *Partisan Review*. Then an English publisher agreed to bring out *Giovanni's Room* for a $400 advance. This aroused the interest of a U.S. publisher, Dial Press, which offered Baldwin a $2,000 contract. Both publishers seemed not to have been as fearful of legal problems due to the subject matter as Knopf and others had been.

When *Giovanni's Room* appeared, the reviews were favorable. The *New York Times* reviewer said James had handled a sensitive subject with "dignity and intensity," while another reviewer called the novel "nearly heroic." And in the *Nation*, National Book Award winner Nelson Algren said that *Giovanni's Room* was written with "driving intensity and horror sustained all the way."[18]

Nevertheless, there were protests about the subject matter. Some readers, white and black, felt homosexuality was obscene and should not be written about at all. There were blacks who felt that since he had established himself as a spokesperson on race in *Notes of a Native Son*, it was not fitting that he should write about two gay white men. Blacks had enough troubles without having to deal with implications that the writer who pleaded their cause was gay.

There were also gay people who objected to the book because the openly gay Giovanni dies a horrible death at the end of the novel while the narrator, who has denied his feelings for another man, goes on living. And there were those who said that Baldwin had written the book only because the subject had shock value and shock value had dollar value and that meant more sales and more money for the author.

Baldwin himself had only one answer for all of his critics. *Giovanni's Room,* he said, is "not about homosexual love. It's about what happens to you if you're afraid to love anybody."[19]

SIX

The Civil Rights Struggle

uring the time that James had been busy writing and publishing *Giovanni's Room,* a series of events affecting blacks in the United States had been shaping the civil rights movement. In January 1955, Marian Anderson became the first African American permitted to sing at the Metropolitan Opera House in New York City. Sixteen years earlier, Ms. Anderson had been barred by the Daughters of the American Revolution from singing at Constitution Hall in Washington because of her color.

Eleanor Roosevelt, wife of the president, had resigned from the organization and arranged an outdoor concert for Ms. Anderson at the Lincoln Memorial. There had been much outrage at the bigotry of the DAR, and yet it had taken these sixteen years for a great singer whose magnificent contralto voice was admired all over the world to be invited to sing at the Met. Blacks in the North, Baldwin would write, "do not escape Jim Crow: they merely encounter another, not-less-deadly variety."[1]

However, it was events in the South, not the North, which stirred Baldwin. One of the first of these was the murder of Emmett Till, a fourteen-year-old boy from Chicago who visited the town of Money, Mississippi, in August 1955. There are differing versions of the events leading up to the killing.

One says that Emmett whistled at a young white woman on the street. Another says that he went into a general store on a dare and asked the white woman behind the counter for a date. According to this account, Emmett called the young woman, who was married, "baby."

There is little doubt about what happened next. That night a group of white men including J. W. Milliam dragged Emmett from his bed and drove him out in the country. They tortured him for several hours. Then Milliam held a gun to Emmett's head and asked the boy if he still thought he was as good as a white man. When Emmett said yes, Milliam shot and killed him. They threw Emmett's body into the river. Later the killers were tried by an all-white jury and acquitted.

Although James knew that killings of black people by white people were all too common in the South of that period, he was nevertheless disgusted by the way Emmett Till's killers had been able to thumb their noses at the justice system. It made him look once again at the conditions under which blacks were forced to live in his native land. The Till case haunted him and eventually it would result in his writing the play *Blues for Mister Charlie* based on it.

Following the Emmett Till murder, the civil rights movement in the South began to pick up momentum. On December 1, 1955, in Montgomery, Alabama, a seamstress named Rosa Parks was seated in the black section of one of the city's legally segregated buses. When the *Whites Only* section of the bus filled up, the driver ordered her to get up and give her seat to a white person.

She refused. Rosa Parks's feet hurt. She didn't want to stand all the way home.

Rosa Parks was arrested. A few days later a young black minister named Martin Luther King Jr. called a meeting of Montgomery's black clergy. They issued a statement protesting the arrest and demanding that the Montgomery bus companies seat people on a first-come first-served basis. Black people would not ride the buses until the bus companies agreed to do this.

That was the beginning of the Montgomery bus boycott. The day it began, only 8 black passengers rode the buses. Normally there would have been some 17,500 black riders. The boycott lasted 381 days. When

Rosa Parks, accompanied by a deputy and a lawyer, goes to jail.

it ended in victory for the blacks of Montgomery, the Reverend King had been established as the leader of a movement that would change the South forever.

In January 1956, during the second month of the boycott, King's home was bombed. He wasn't home, but his wife and baby were. The bomb broke all the front windows of the house and wrecked the living room. His wife grabbed the baby and ran out the back.

According to biographer David Leeming, "Baldwin was acutely aware of the developing civil rights movement in the States and of his distance from it."[2] Also he was coming to realize that he was not just a black man who could have an easier time of it in Europe than in the United States. He was an African *American*. He might hate how blacks were treated in his homeland, but he could no more escape being American than he could escape being black.

This feeling was strengthened when he covered the conference of Negro-African Writers and Artists in Paris for *Encounter* magazine. It showed him that he—and possibly all African Americans—had been shaped by the country in which they lived at least as much (and possibly more) than by the continent from which their ancestors had been kidnapped. The Africans he met at the Conference "hated America." He realized that "whenever I was with an African, we would both be uneasy. . . . The terms of our life were so different, we almost needed a dictionary to talk."[3]

After the conference, the pull James felt to become part of the growing civil rights struggle in America increased. There were clashes occurring all over the South. In the wake of the Supreme Court decision outlawing segregated schools, the University of Alabama had been forced to admit a young black woman named Autherine Lucy. There had been riots and she had been expelled. The university's trustees said they took the action because she had made "outrageous, false and baseless accusations" against college officials.[4]

There was a black boycott of businesses in Tuskeegee, Alabama, to protest white efforts to keep blacks from voting. White Citizens Councils were springing up all over the South to stop the nonviolent integration movement headed by Dr. King. A newly built public school in Nashville, Tennessee, was destroyed by dynamite after registering its first black child. In Charlotte, North Carolina, a fifteen-year-old black girl trying to enter a formerly all-white school was set upon by whites.

Strolling down the Boulevard St. Germain in Paris, James Baldwin spied a newspaper with a front-page picture of the frightened girl backing away from the jeering, spitting mob. For a long time afterward, he could not get that picture out of his mind. How could he remain here safely in France when schoolchildren were fighting for black civil rights—*his* civil rights—back home?

This was his struggle as much as it was theirs. He had to be a part of it. James made arrangements to leave Paris and go home. He arrived in New York in July 1957.

Soon after he returned home, James got assignments from *Harper's Magazine* and *Partisan Review* to write articles on the civil right struggle. With his expenses covered, James headed south.

Pictures of African-Americans breaking down segregation, like this one, forced Baldwin to return to the United States.

"The South had always frightened me," James would write. Now "I wondered where children got their strength . . . to walk through mobs to get to school."[5]

Pictures of children doing that in Little Rock, Arkansas, filled the nation's newspapers and dominated the TV news. When an attempt was made to enroll black children in Little Rock's Central High School, the children were met by an unruly white mob spitting on them and throwing rocks and yelling "Go home, niggers!" The governor of the state, Orville Faubus, claiming that the confrontation was becoming "more explosive by the hour," sent in the state militia to stop the black children from entering the school. This was a direct violation of federal law and was denounced by Little Rock's mayor, Woodrow Mann. "If any racial trouble does develop," the mayor stated with some bitterness, "the blame rests squarely on the doorstep of the governor's mansion."[6]

Of course trouble did develop. With the arrival of the militia the white civilian mob grew from 400 to 1,500 and became unmanageable. Finally, President Dwight D. Eisenhower directed Governor Faubus to obey "the supreme law of the land" and withdraw the state militia from Little Rock.[7] They were replaced by federal troops—armed paratroopers who escorted the nine black children into the school each day.

Although he followed events there closely, James was not in Little Rock. Instead, he was in Charlotte, North Carolina. He had wanted to go to Charlotte since the picture of the black girl trying to integrate the white school there had stirred his conscience and brought him back to the United States from France.

Her name was Dorothy Counts, and she was the daughter of a black minister. "After several days of being stoned and spat on by the mob," Baldwin wrote, she "had withdrawn from Harding High," one of the all-white schools that the federal courts had directed to admit black students. As a result of the court order, "Charlotte, a town of 165,000, was in a ferment when I was there because of its 50,000 Negroes, four had been assigned to all-white schools, one to each school."[8]

In his article, James tried to get across why education was so important to the black parents of Charlotte that they would risk their children's safety for it. "Those Negro parents who spend their days trembling for their children and the rest of their time praying that their children have not been too badly damaged inside, are not doing this out of 'ideals' or 'convictions' or because they are in the grip of a perverse desire to send their children where 'they are not wanted,'" he pointed out. "They are doing it because they want the child to receive the education which will allow him to defeat, possibly escape, and not impossibly help one day abolish the stifling environment in which they see, daily, so many children perish."[9]

Segregation was the traditional way of life in Charlotte. "Negroes there are not even licensed to become electricians or plumbers," James observed. Sarcastically, he added that he had been told by white people that race relations in Charlotte were "excellent," but that "I failed to find a single Negro who agreed with this."[10]

If this was how it was in the South, James wondered, what could it be like in the Deep South? His next stop was Atlanta, Georgia, the city which—thanks to the film *Gone with the Wind*—most symbolized the Confederacy. Atlanta, James would observe, had "a very bitter interracial history."[11]

In Atlanta, James experienced Jim Crow personally when his color dictated that he must ride in the back of a city bus. For most black people in Atlanta such segregation was a part of daily life. Yet not all Atlanta blacks were in favor of the efforts to bring integration to the buses and schools and lunch counters of their city.

James wrote of discovering "a prosperous black community that was somewhat isolated from the rest of the black population."[12] These people did not usually ride the buses. They owned their own cars and drove them to work. They thought that actions taken by Atlanta's civil rights movement were "bad for business." When James reported this in his article for *Partisan Review*, he was accused of exaggeration and of undermining efforts by some black community leaders to work with whites to integrate Atlanta peacefully.

Peaceful integration was the aim of the Southern Christian Leadership Conference headed by Dr. Martin Luther King Jr. Nonviolence and passive resistance were key elements in their push for integration. So too were protests and boycotts and marches and sit-ins.

James met Dr. King for the first time in Atlanta. The Reverend, whose father was also a minister, was in the city to visit his parents. James was tremendously impressed by the inner conviction that shone through King's quiet explanation of how the teachings of Mohandas K. Gandhi—leader of the nonviolent independence movement that had driven the British out of India—had inspired him to organize a crusade to confront segregation in the South. The depth of Dr. King's convictions lent the man moral authority which James would come to believe could not be denied.

When Dr. King flew back to Montgomery, Alabama, James followed. He found Montgomery a city in the throes of profound change. He could feel the hostility from many whites toward blacks. At the

Martin Luther King Jr. (standing) advocated nonviolent resistance to racist institutions and laws.

same time, he could feel the pride of blacks boarding a bus and sitting down in what had once been the "whites only" section.

That pride was expressed as a kind of joy that filled the Dexter Avenue Baptist Church, which James attended on Sunday. When Dr. King spoke, his simple sermon urging the members of the congregation to join in the struggle for civil rights turned that joy into a group commitment to support the crusade. His voice, so quiet during his one-on-one conversation with James, was like thunder from the pulpit—a wake-up call to all America which could not be denied.

James was deeply moved. Not just the magnetism of Dr. King, but all of what he experienced on this first southern trip convinced him that he had a duty to make as many Americans as possible aware of the heroic struggle being waged by those fighting for equality. He viewed it as a mission and that came through in the articles he wrote reporting on this journey through the South and others that followed.

His articles were very well received. Readers began identifying James with the struggle about which he was reporting. His passionate writing made them see—perhaps even feel—what it was like to be a black standing up to segregation in the South. He was a major force in shaping public opinion in the North to favor those fighting for equality in the South.

But when James turned his attention to segregation in the North— well, that would be another matter entirely.

"Another Country"

n early 1960 *Esquire* magazine hired James Baldwin to do a piece on Harlem. For more than two years James had been devoting himself to traveling through the South writing articles about the civil rights struggle and to working on a new novel, *Another Country.* Now he was being asked to look at African Americans' most famous community in the North. But when "Fifth Avenue Uptown: A Letter from Harlem" was published in the July issue of *Esquire,* there were protests from all sides.

The long article detailed the poverty and the hopelessness of Harlem. It portrayed the slum housing, the uncollected garbage, the decaying streets. It described the drug problem—serious, but by no means as widespread then as it is today—and its fallout.

He exposed the white slumlords who "make a tidy profit by raising the rent, chopping up the rooms, and all but dispensing with the upkeep."[1] He described the white police who patrolled the streets of Harlem "like an occupying soldier in a bitterly hostile country."[2] He discussed how white storekeepers charged Harlem blacks more for food and other merchandise than white customers in white neighborhoods paid.

But James was no more sparing of blacks in Harlem. He pointed a disapproving finger at black drug kingpins, black gangsters, and black

Baldwin stands in front of a Harlem slum.

gamblers preying on their fellow blacks, and at the teenage black van-
dals who destroyed the housing projects, which perhaps deserved to be
destroyed because, James claimed, they were designed more like jails
than like decent living quarters. "Walk through the streets of Harlem,"
James wrote, "and see what we, this nation, have become."[3]

Many hardworking blacks who lived in Harlem and brought up families there were hurt by his portrayal of their neighborhood. They felt that
he had concentrated on the downside and ignored the churches and festi-
vals and music of Harlem, the vibrancy and spirit of its people. The resi-
dents of Riverton, the housing project he described as "a slum," were
outraged and demanded an apology from him. James would not apologize, but he was saddened that he might have added to their misery.

At the same time, Harlem's white shopkeepers objected that James had done them an injustice. "Go shopping one day in Harlem," he had written, "and compare Harlem quality and prices with those downtown."[4] The quality, the storekeepers pointed out, was what the neighborhood could afford. And if the prices were slightly higher, that was because it cost more to do business in Harlem than in neighborhoods where people paid cash for items rather than paying out the cost over a period of time, and because there was more shoplifting in poor areas like Harlem than in middle-class neighborhoods.

New York whites generally reacted to the article with disbelief. City spokespersons accused James of exaggerating the poverty of Harlem. They could not believe the depth of the antiwhite sentiment he revealed. They pointed out how much better off the blacks of Harlem and the North generally were than those in the segregated South.

James wasn't so sure. He had touched a sore spot when he wrote in his article that Northerners think "that they can ignore what is happening in Northern cities because what is happening in Little Rock or Birmingham is worse."[5] Comparing the clear-cut segregation of the South with the inconsistent and murky bigotry of the North, he pointed out that there were blacks who preferred the South because "at least there you haven't got to play any guessing games."[6] He said that African Americans were "ignored in the North and are under surveillance in the South, and suffer hideously in both places."[7]

The uproar died down only to be revived a year later when James's article was reprinted in his second book of essays, *Nobody Knows My Name.* Again there were demands that James apologize for his portrait of Harlem and again he refused. He felt that while the South was in turmoil, it was changing. But northern black ghettoes were getting worse, and the problem was being ignored. James felt a writer's obligation to truth and a duty to help black people face it even when they resented him for it.

His third novel, *Another Country,* was published in the summer of 1962. It was set in Greenwich Village in the mid-1950s. The characters were blacks and whites, straights and gays, writers and musicians and actors, hustlers and failures. The structure was loose, with multiple plot lines and conflicts that were not always resolved. The love scenes were between men and women and between people of the same sex, between couples of the same color and between those of different races, between unmarried lovers and married couples, and between those who were married but not to each other.

The scenes were not shocking by today's standards. The lovemaking was not described in detail. Nevertheless, at the time there were many objections that *Another Country* was obscene. The review by Stanley Edgar Hyman in the *New Leader*, characterizing *Another Country* as "pornography" and "degrading" was typical of some of the moral outrage that greeted the publication of the novel.[8] Defending his book, James noted that "in most of the novels written by Negroes until today . . . there is a great space where sex ought to be; and what usually fills this space is violence."[9]

Another Country was not violent, but it did have "power," according to eminent critic Lionel Trilling. In his review he compared James to one of America's greatest writers, Theodore Dreiser. The piece by Langston Hughes for *Kirkus Reviews* also praised the novel's "certain emotional power." Even Norman Mailer, who didn't like *Another Country*, wrote that it was "a powerful book."[10]

But Mailer was troubled by its structure, observing that "Baldwin commits every *gaffe* in the art of novel writing."[11] Other reviewers also were disturbed by the rambling nature of the narrative, the unresolved plot lines, and the lack of resolution of the moral questions raised.

Baldwin himself admitted that there was some justice to these criticisms but believed the reviewers had not grasped the intention behind the looseness of the writing. He had deliberately written *Another Country* in the style of a jazz or blues improvisation. The novel's episodes were thematic riffs, part of the music of life which is not always smooth and often does merely trail off rather than end in a well-arranged finale.

In an article for the *New York Times Book Review*, James wrote, "I would like to think that some of the people who liked [*Another Country*] responded to it in the way they respond when Miles [Davis] and Ray [Charles] are blowing." His book was intended, like the music of the two famous African-American musicians, to "sing a kind of universal blues."[12]

Despite the criticism, *Another Country* was an immediate best-seller. Indeed, when the paperback edition came out a year later, it sold more copies than any other paperback of 1963 with the exception of *Lord of the Flies*. No doubt word of mouth of the novel's supposedly daring sex scenes ran up sales.

This reputation would cling to the book even after American attitudes toward sex became much more liberal. As late as 1968 the University of Montana banished the novel from the classroom and the teacher who had attempted to read from it was labeled a "smut peddler."[13] Even today, when *Another Country* is recommended reading at many colleges, it is banned at some schools.

During the period immediately following the publication of *Another Country*, there were frequent attempts to stop its distribution. In New Orleans a bookstore owner was arrested for disregarding "city ordinances pertaining to the sale of obscene literature" by displaying *Another Country*. Calling the book "sex perversion at its vilest," an outraged citizen wrote from Fort Worth, Texas, to J. Edgar Hoover, head of the Federal Bureau of Investigation, protesting the novel's availability in a local drugstore and demanding that the FBI take action to prevent further sales of it.[14]

The FBI, however, was already looking into whether *Another Country* should be banned nationwide, along with other novels, such as Henry Miller's *Tropic of Cancer*, that were judged to have erotic content. They also had a file on James Baldwin himself. It contained entries on his activities, his friends and associates, and his family.

The FBI had put James under surveillance in earnest from his first trip south and his first meeting with Dr. Martin Luther King Jr., on whom they were also keeping a file. During the time of the civil rights struggle it was common practice for the FBI to track the activities of the movement's leaders. At first this was done out of concern that the Communists might try to take over groups which were active in seeking equality for African Americans. These included activist organizations like the Southern Christian Leadership Conference (SCLC), the Student Nonviolent Coordinating Committee (SNCC), and the Congress of Racial Equality (CORE).

The focus shifted when the J. Edgar Hoover began to see danger in the organizations themselves. They were changing society, and in Hoover's view, to the extent that they succeeded, they were a threat to the stability of the nation. The FBI redoubled its surveillance efforts, concentrating on those they perceived as leaders of the movement.

They saw James as one of these leaders. His writings about Dr. King, the various civil rights organizations, and their activities made him a leader in the FBI's eyes, despite his own belief that he was not. There was no denying the influence of his writings, and the FBI kept a careful eye on them as well as on James himself.

Since James was an admirer of Dr. King, what he had written thus far had been in the same vein as Dr. King's nonviolent teachings. James had reported on and admired the techniques of passive resistance used by the movement. But that was about to change. The FBI was about to have reason to view James as extremely dangerous.

He was about to publish his most controversial book. The FBI, many white people, and some black people were not going to like it. The book would raise the possibility of race violence in America on an unthinkable scale. It would be called *The Fire Next Time*.

EIGHT

"The Fire Next Time"

"**T**he white man is the devil!"[1] **This was the message** preached by the Honorable Elijah Muhammed, leader of the Nation of Islam. The Nation had been founded in Detroit in the early 1930s by Wallace Fard, a follower of the Back to Africa movement started by Marcus Garvey. Many blacks in the 1920s had agreed with Garvey's message that their only hope was to leave white America and return to the land of their black ancestors. In 1934, Fard mysteriously disappeared, and the Honorable Elijah Muhammed became the group's leader. In 1936, he founded the Chicago Temple, which became the headquarters for the Nation of Islam.

By 1962 the Chicago Temple had grown and expanded to other cities. The Honorable Elijah Muhammed was still its leader. That was the year James Baldwin wrote a lengthy account for the *New Yorker* magazine on Muhammed and his followers, who were known as Black Muslims. The article, "The Fire Next Time," was also published as a book with the same title.

At the end of September 1962, while James had been working on the article, a massive riot had broken out at the University of Mississippi. Three people had been killed, fifty injured, two hundred arrested. The cause of the riot was an attempt by a young black student,

Elijah Muhammed became the subject of several Baldwin articles.

James Meredith, to register at the school. Obeying the law, the university's board of trustees had allowed Meredith to enroll. But Mississippi governor Ross Barnett had ordered state troopers to prevent Meredith from attending classes.

Trying to cool down the situation, President John F. Kennedy made a plea to the people of Mississippi to stay calm. The speech was obviously meant for the whites of Mississippi who were threatening Meredith—spitting on him and throwing rocks at him—while the state troopers stood by and watched. Baldwin was outraged. He said Kennedy's speech sounded "as if there were no Negroes" in Mississippi. He called the speech "shameful."[2] President Kennedy eventually sent in U.S. troops to enable Meredith to attend classes. That's when the riot really exploded.

When *The Fire Next Time* was published in book form early in 1963, it drew white America's attention to the Nation of Islam for the second time. The first time had been a few years earlier when Mike Wallace made a TV documentary about them called "The Hate That Hate Produced." It had caused widespread alarm about the antiwhite speeches of the group's leaders and their talk of violence against whites.

The Nation might have been dismissed as a lunatic-fringe group by most whites at the time, but one man prevented that. He was the most famous Black Muslim, second in power only to the Honorable Elijah Muhammed and already better known to whites than the leader of the Nation of Islam. He had charisma, was a tremendously effective speaker, and had brought many young black men into the Nation. He called himself Malcolm X.

"White people need someone to tell them what time it is," Malcolm had told the television audience. Blacks, he added, must claim what is rightfully theirs "by any means necessary."[3]

Malcolm's message was the flip side of the nonviolence and passive resistance preached by the Reverend Martin Luther King Jr. The

Malcolm X became a voice for black fury and protest.

members of the Nation of Islam did not believe in turning the other cheek. On the contrary, they believed in an eye for an eye.

James had seen Malcolm's followers handing out their literature and speaking from soapboxes on the street corners of Harlem. The men all dressed the same with dark blue suits, starched white shirts, and conservative ties, and all had short, neat haircuts. They always drew a large crowd. "The white man's Heaven is the black man's Hell!" they would proclaim, and the crowd would murmur, or sometimes shout "Amen to that!"[4]

It wasn't a message James could embrace. He didn't believe things were that simple. But one night he noticed something that had nothing to do with the message, but which impressed him: the police were behaving differently. "I had seen men dragged from their platforms for saying less virulent things, and I had seen many crowds dispersed by policemen, with clubs or on horseback. But the policemen were doing nothing now," he would write. James realized it was "because they were afraid." Having been badly treated by the police on occasion himself, he added, "I was delighted to see it."[5]

James included this incident in *The Fire Next Time* to show the extent to which the Nation of Islam built confidence in its young followers. The white police could not scare them, and when the police realized that, they themselves were frightened. This was a mighty message in Harlem where the police frightened everyone.

The Black Muslims were small in number, but the black people who admired them and their message were not. The message was that whites had risen on the backs of blacks and that the time was at hand for whites to fall. To ignore this prophecy, James believed, would be to suffer its consequences. James saw it as his task to impress the full meaning of this warning on the white world. That was the theme of *The Fire Next Time*.

James might never have written the book had he not by mid-1961 become known as an outspoken supporter of the nonviolent civil rights movement which was so different from Black Muslim beliefs. Because James and Malcolm X represented opposing points of view, they were asked to appear on a television program together. The Honorable Elijah Muhammed saw the show and invited James to visit him.

So on an August evening in 1961, James went to Muhammed's home in Chicago. He was nervous. He knew that he would not be able to smoke, nor be offered a drink with liquor in it. Black Muslims did not use tobacco, or liquor, or drugs. They did not approve of sex outside of marriage. They considered homosexuality a sin. James had, of course, been guilty of all these things and in the eyes of the leader of the Nation of Islam, he must have been considered unclean.

Nevertheless, James reported, Elijah Muhammed welcomed him with a "marvellous smile." "I was drawn toward his peculiar authority," James would admit. "He made me think of my father and me as we might have been if we had been friends."[6]

Followers of the Honorable Elijah Muhammed were also present. Whenever he made a point, "a kind of chorus arose from the table saying 'Yes, that's right.' This began to set my teeth on edge," James reported.[7] It made it harder to disagree with the Black Muslim leader.

Still, James could not agree. Most of Elijah Muhammed's points had their basis in his belief that the white man was evil and must be destroyed. He had much evidence of white wickedness toward blacks which James could not deny. Elijah Muhammed believed, therefore, that on the Day of Judgement all blacks would be saved and all whites would perish. He also mentioned that marriage, love, or sex between whites and blacks was a very great sin.

"I felt that I was back in my father's house," James wrote. "I told Elijah that I did not care if white and black people married, and that I had many white friends. I would have no choice, if it came to it, but to perish with them." And James wondered what would happen if "I love a few people and they love me and some of them are white, and isn't love more important than color?"[8]

"The Fire Next Time" appeared in the *New Yorker* in November 1962. In January 1963, it came out in book form. In the two months between, it "really caused a sensation" according to William Shawn, editor in chief of the *New Yorker.* Shawn added that Baldwin "had been saying things that hadn't been said before. And everybody was talking about it."[9]

Quite a bit of the talk condemned the article and then the book. There were complaints that it made people take Malcolm X too seriously. The book had dealt far more with the Honorable Elijah Muhammed than with Malcolm, but it was Malcolm who was the fiery activist who generated fear. He was an ex-convict, critics of *The Fire Next Time* pointed out, a rabblerouser. And James, by his respectful treatment of the Black Muslims, was giving Malcolm an importance he didn't deserve.

But James, like Malcolm, had been raised in black slums. He knew what that could do and how easily it could lead to a jail cell. He understood the depth of the black anger, which responded to Malcolm and the Black Muslim beliefs. James understood why black separation and war against whites might appeal more to many black people than the civil rights movement. Whatever else it stood for, the Nation of Islam offered blacks the dignity whites denied them.

James wanted whites to understand this so that they would see how important it was to support nonviolent actions for equality. Whites had to be made aware that there continued to be much truth behind the Black Muslim view of white America as a decaying society unwilling to change its bigoted ways. He had written *The Fire Next Time* to tell them this before it was too late.

White America was shocked. The depths of black anger revealed by *The Fire Next Time* seemed terribly at odds with the civil rights movement—and James was identified with the movement. Even as the book was hailed for its power and insight, there were doubts about its message. Before very long, however, the accuracy of its prophecy would make it a classic.

Shortly after the book was published, James went to Jackson, Mississippi, to meet with Medgar Evers, the head of the Jackson chapter of the National Association for the Advancement of Colored People. Evers was trying to bring charges against a local white storekeeper who had killed a black man. This meant going into isolated woodlands to search for evidence. Since Evers was a target for certain white men who didn't want the storekeeper punished, this was very dangerous. James went with Evers on one of these trips. "He had the calm of somebody who knows he's going to die," Baldwin observed.[10] Evers was murdered three months later in the driveway of his home.

While James was in Mississippi, the state of Alabama was exploding. Dr. King, leading protest marches in Birmingham demanding more jobs for blacks and desegregation of public rest rooms and restaurants, had been arrested three times by Sheriff Bull Connor. The sheriff's men had repeatedly clubbed the demonstrators. When local black youngsters organized a Children's Crusade, Connor turned fire hoses and police dogs on them. Over a thousand demonstrators were beaten and arrested. The nightly TV news was filled with pictures of bleeding black children.

On May 11, 1963, Dr. King's Birmingham offices were firebombed. Outraged, Baldwin sent a telegram to Attorney General Robert Kennedy demanding that the president take action. Instead, President Kennedy asked blacks to halt the demonstrations so that there might be a cooling-off period. Dr. King protested that what the president was suggesting was "too little, too late." Shortly before this, the president had criticized the Black Muslims as an extremist group. Now Malcolm X exploded. "Instead of attacking the Ku Klux Klan and the White Citizens' Committee," he fumed, "Kennedy attacked Islam, a religion."[11]

It didn't escape James's attention that Dr. King and Malcolm X had both reacted with disapproval to the president's suggestion. He hoped that others might see that despite the difference in their tactics, both men were voicing the attitude of most blacks in America. And in his way, James too was delivering the message that change must come—and come quickly.

His role as a spokesperson impressed *Time* magazine. On May 17, 1963, James Baldwin's picture appeared on the cover of *Time*. The text inside paid tribute to his words and actions in the struggle for civil rights.

A week later Attorney General Robert Kennedy asked James to gather a group of prominent blacks to meet with him to discuss the struggle for black equality. The meeting took place in New York City. Kennedy and the other white officials talked in terms of reforming the existing system. The blacks—including Baldwin, psychologist Kenneth Clark, Harry Belafonte, Lena Horne, and playwright Lorraine Hansberry—wanted the government to enforce civil rights with whatever force was necessary. But

Baldwin met two friends, Marlon Brando (right of Baldwin) and Charlton Heston (left of Baldwin), at the March on Washington, 1963.

they could not make the whites understand that the time for compromise and nonviolence was running out.

For the next two months, James was involved in planning a march on Washington to demand that Congress pass a civil rights bill. The August 28 march was a great success. It drew a quarter of a million people, the largest protest of its kind in the history of the capital. The Reverend Martin Luther King Jr. delivered his famous "I have a dream" speech and the crowd joined Joan Baez in singing "We Shall Overcome."

But not everybody was happy about the march. Congressional leaders doubted that it would influence passage of a civil rights bill. Malcolm X called it the "farce on Washington." He advised blacks "to get yourself a .45 and then start singing 'We Shall Overcome.' "[12]

Eighteen days after the march, on a Sunday morning in Birmingham, Alabama, a bomb was thrown into a black church during services. Four

**Baldwin wore this arm band to protest
the Birmingham Church bombing.**

little girls were killed. Black rage could not be contained. During the riots which followed, two young black boys were shot to death.

"Why be non-violent," Malcolm asked, "when they bomb your churches and kill your children?"[13] And James, who had always supported nonviolence and whose message had always been love, could not stop himself from pointing out that "the only time that non-violence has been admired is when Negroes practice it."[14]

But his bitterness would not be permanent. James was not Malcolm. He could not live by violence. "If you give people hatred," he would write in his novel *If Beale Street Could Talk*, "they will give it back to you."[15]

James had not always turned the other cheek, nor would he. But he would always know deep down that hatred canceled out hope. Hope could only survive where there was love to feed it.

N I N E

Caught in the Middle

On April 23, 1964, James Baldwin's second play, *Blues for Mister Charlie*, opened on Broadway. It was dedicated to the memory of the four little girls killed in the church bombing, to the other murdered children of Birmingham, and to the slain civil rights leader Medgar Evers. It was loosely based on the Emmet Till case, and James's brother David was in the cast.

Much of the play had been written on buses and trains on the way to civil rights meetings and protests. During the mid-1960s James's involvement in the movement took up more and more of his time. This was not just a matter of writing, or making speeches, or participating in planning sessions and other meetings, but also of putting himself in harm's way in the front lines of the struggle.

The bitterness James felt about the treatment of African Americans in his native land runs all through *Blues for Mister Charlie*. Because of this, some critics thought that his role as a civil rights spokesperson was interfering with his talent as a writer. Other reviewers, however, were deeply moved by his angry message. One review by David Boroff in the *National Observer* seems to sum up both views. "Mr. Baldwin," wrote Boroff, "has written a raw, stinging denunciation of racial oppression." He went on to say that the play was "militantly propagandistic in intent, often crudely oversimplified, but unfailingly vivid, moving, and powerful."[1]

The play was harsh, to say the least, in its expression of black feelings toward white people. "I hope I'm pregnant," says one character after her lover has been killed by whites. "One more illegitimate black baby—that's right you jive mothers!"[2] Just before the curtain falls, the focus is on the black hero's Bible as it is raised to reveal a gun under it.

It had not been James's purpose to advocate violence, but rather to reveal what might drive blacks to it. He did not agree with the anti-white positions taken by Malcolm X and other black militants, but he did fully understand their causes. The voice in the play that was more truly James's voice belonged to the minister father of the murdered hero. "Teach us to trust the great gift of life," he preaches, "and learn to love one another and dare to walk the earth like men. Amen."[3]

This was a very different message from that of Malcolm, and James was always amazed when his critics treated his depictions of black anger as if he was recommending the violence of the feelings he portrayed.

In March 1964, James was surprised when Malcolm announced that he was leaving the Nation of Islam to form his own Black Nationalist Party. But leaving the Nation did not soften Malcolm's activism. "I shall tell [Negroes] what a real revolution means," he announced. "There can be no revolution without bloodshed, and it is nonsense to describe the civil rights movement as a revolution."[4]

James, of course, did not feel that way. However, when there was a series of relatively small (compared to what would come later) race riots in northern American cities like New York, Rochester, Paterson, and Elizabeth beginning in 1964, he was identified with them because of his predictions in *The Fire Next Time*. At the same time he was being criticized by black activist-writers like Amiri Baraka (then known as Leroi Jones) for being too tolerant of whites.

It was a confused time, not just for James, but for the nation. Blacks had long been denied the vote in the South, and at the beginning of 1965, the Reverend Martin Luther King Jr. had organized demonstrations in Selma, Alabama, to force authorities there to register black citizens to vote. On February 10, Dr. King and 770 others were arrested for picketing a county courthouse. Two days later, over 1,000 black schoolchildren were arrested. Pictures of them being herded into a makeshift jail by deputies using cattle prods and swinging clubs dominated the news on TV.

At this time James was in London meeting with British philosopher Bertrand Russell. He had come to discuss joining a war crimes tribunal Russell was starting to condemn United States actions in Vietnam. The meeting took place at the very beginning of what become known as the Vietnam War.

Before World War II, Vietnam had been a French colony. After the war the Vietnamese had rebelled against the French and driven them out. A 1954 peace settlement had divided the nation into two parts, the northern half under the control of a Communist military which had been the major force against the French, the southern half under a succession of nondemocratic anti-Communist governments friendly to the United States. It had been agreed that the country would be reunified in 1956 following an election in which all the citizens, north and south, would decide who would rule Vietnam.

The election never took place. It was blocked by the South Vietnamese government with the active support of the United States, which feared that the Communists might win. The U.S. government was afraid that if all of Vietnam came under Communist rule, Communism would spread to Laos, Cambodia, and the rest of Southeast Asia. Even the Philippines might fall to the Communists.

With the elections canceled, North Vietnamese troops moved into position to invade South Vietnam. The United States sent military advisers to help organize and train a South Vietnamese army. In August 1964, following an unconfirmed report that North Vietnamese patrol boats had fired on U.S. warships in the Gulf of Tonkin, a resolution was passed in Congress authorizing the president to take "all necessary action" to defend U.S. forces.[5] Soon thereafter, U.S. warplanes began bombing North Vietnam.

The situation escalated rapidly. By April 1965 the first American combat troops had landed in Vietnam. It was the beginning of a very bloody war, and already there were Americans and others around the world who protested the United States' role in it. James Baldwin was one of those who had opposed the war even before the troops landed.

From the first he believed that money being spent on government programs to help African Americans would be diverted to pay for the war. When it became obvious that more and more young blacks from low-income families would be doing the fighting in Vietnam while white middle-class college students remained safely at home, he was outraged. Why, James would ask, should America "liberate" South Vietnam when it could not liberate its own black people? He declared the "American Adventure in Vietnam a desperate and despicable folly."[6]

While James was in London, he heard the news that Malcolm X had been murdered. James had always liked Malcolm personally and admired his forcefulness even as he disagreed with his antiwhite views. Most recently, when Malcolm had returned from a Muslim pilgrimage to announce that he no longer believed all whites were devils, James applauded his courage.

James regarded Malcolm's change of heart so positively that he had agreed to a meeting with him and with Dr. Martin Luther King Jr. for the purpose of enlisting Malcolm's energy in the twin causes of integration and civil rights. Now that meeting would never take place. Malcolm had been gunned down by Black Muslims as he rose to make a speech in the Audubon Ballroom in Harlem.

The day after the murder James flew back to New York City. Reporters met his plane and asked for comments on the murder of Malcolm X by black men. "The hand that pulled the trigger did not buy the bullet," Baldwin told them. "That bullet was forged in the crucible of the Western world."[7]

A little more than two weeks after the murder of Malcolm X, the voting rights protests in Selma, Alabama, were put down with such brutality by the local police that eighty marchers were hospitalized. Network TV interrupted programs so that all America might view the carnage which came to be known as Bloody Sunday. President Johnson went before Congress to announce his support for a voting rights bill, and at the same time Dr. King announced that he would lead a march from Selma to Montgomery, the capital of Alabama, to demand that the state government safeguard the rights of Selma blacks to register to vote.

James Baldwin joined the protesters on the outskirts of Montgomery. He and 40,000 others marched through a driving rainstorm into the city. The next day at a ballpark rally filled with celebrities, James was one of many who briefly spoke to the crowd.

He supported Dr. King. At the same time James was torn by the violence which seemed so much more in evidence than nonviolence. In the short time since the killing of Malcolm there had been two cold-blooded murders of civil rights supporters in Alabama. The Unitarian minister Reverend James Reeb had been beaten to death by hoodlums in Selma, and Detroit housewife-activist Viola Liuzzo had been shot and killed while driving freedom marchers outside Montgomery. These deaths had followed close on the heels of the murders of three civil rights workers in Mississippi—southern black James Chaney and northern white Jews Michael Schwerner and Andrew Goodman.

The ongoing violence raised doubts in James's mind about the tactics of Dr. King. According to his biographer David Leeming, he "was frustrated with the civil rights movement itself." Like some of the younger black leaders, he worried that the movement was dominated by nonmilitant whites. He had become impatient with Dr. King's commitment to turning the other cheek. Without attacking Dr. King and his philosophy directly as some others would soon do, James questioned it indirectly. "If you're frightened of something in the streets you walk towards it," James pointed out. "Turn your back and they've got you."[8]

But James was linked with Dr. King not only by his commitment to civil rights but also by his opposition to the Vietnam War. Like King, he had been criticized by movement allies for this. They felt that antiwar organizations were drawing off the energy of white liberals and that financial support was being lost to the antiwar crusade.

Even as he opposed the war, James understood the bitterness of militant blacks. To them the struggle was very personal and its outcome would directly affect them and their children. They could not walk away from oppression to join a different movement that had become more fashionable. This was their struggle and when liberal whites deserted it, or even when they stayed to try to influence its policy and see that it remained nonviolent, black resentment was inevitable.

This resentment exploded not in the South and in the movement, but rather in the West and in the inner city. Whites, James had written in *The Fire Next Time*, "have destroyed and are destroying hundreds of thousands of lives and do not know it and do not want to know it."[9] Now the Watts neighborhood of Los Angeles made sure that whites not only knew what they had done but also knew the consequences.

Watts was truly a ghetto, a run-down and poverty-stricken all-black section of Los Angeles. The young blacks there had constant run-ins with the white Los Angeles police and there were frequent charges of brutality. In August 1965 the police arrested an African-American man on drunken driving charges. According to black witnesses, the police beat him.

It was the spark that lit the inferno. Angry blacks confronted the police. The mob grew. Windows were broken. A fire was set, and then another. Then all Watts seemed to go up in flames as black teenagers stood watching the blaze and chanting "Burn, baby, burn!"[10] The police sent in riot-control squads, but the anger could not be contained. In the end the governor of California had to provide federal troops to restore peace.

The Watts riot lasted six days. Thirty-four people were killed, and over one thousand were injured. Arrests totaled almost four thousand.

James had ended *The Fire Next Time* with a quote from a slave song derived from the story of Noah's ark and the flood in the Bible. "God gave Noah the rainbow sign. No more water, the fire next time!"[11] he had written. Watts told America that "next time" was today and not tomorrow.

In the wake of Watts there was new interest in *The Fire Next Time*. There was another printing and sales went up. At the same time there were those who thought the book had encouraged young blacks to riot and that James had some responsibility for the devastation of Watts. Many people identified him with the more militant black leaders.

Meanwhile, a battle had been shaping up in the civil rights move-ment between those committed to nonviolence and younger, more militant activists. Dr. King's leadership was beginning to be challenged. Events came to a head in June 1966.

James Meredith, the young black man who had integrated the University of Mississippi, had been shot in the back while on a civil rights "walk against fear" across the state of Mississippi.[12] Civil rights leaders, including Dr. King, Stokely Carmichael of the Student Nonviolent Coordinating Committee (SNCC), and Floyd McKissick of the Congress of Racial Equality (CORE), organized a march to complete Meredith's walk.

Dr. King led the march, and as it passed through the small towns of Mississippi, he was hailed as a great leader. Blacks stood along the roadside in the blazing sun just to catch a glimpse of him. However, among many of the marchers from SNCC and CORE he was sneered at. There was a growing feeling that the days of "black and white together" were over.[13] It came to a head when the march reached Greenwood and Stokely Carmichael was arrested for putting up tents in a black schoolyard. After his release, he addressed the marchers:

"I ain't going to jail no more!" he told the crowd. "The only way we gonna stop them white men from whuppin' us is to take over. We been saying freedom for six years and we ain't got nothin'. What we gonna start sayin' now is Black Power!"[14]

And the crowd roared back in unison: "BLACK POWER! BLACK POWER! BLACK POWER!"

King's reaction was disapproving. "I'm not going to use violence, no matter who says so!" he told reporters.[15]

James, however, disagreed with Dr. King. He spoke up in support of Black Power. He said it was in keeping with the principles of "the self-determination of peoples."[16] Nevertheless, James found himself under attack by advocates of Black Power. Black Panther leader Eldridge Cleaver accused him of a "shameful, sycophantic love of whites."[17] Amiri Baraka pronounced Baldwin's writings "white-tainted."[18]

In December James published a book of short stories, *Going to Meet the Man*. Most critics panned the collection. Once again they thought that some of James's stories suffered from his commitment to civil

**Young black militants, such as Stokely Carmichael, grew
impatient with King's nonviolent approach to change.**

rights. They thought he was too harsh in directing blame toward white
people.

James, it seemed, was caught between a rock and a hard place. The
Black Power activists thought him too prowhite and not militant
enough. Yet many critics saw him as antiwhite and advocating violence.
In reality, his position in the movement, while never extreme, did be-
come more militant as northern cities like Chicago, Cleveland, and New
York erupted with violence. As early as July 1966, James had written
in the *Nation* that "to respect the law, in the context in which the
American Negro finds himself, is simply to surrender his self-respect."[19]

This was not a call to violence, but a warning that violence—particularly police brutality—when used against blacks would be met in kind.
Early in 1968, something terrible happened that caused James to reex-

amine his militancy and to find the words to express his own lifelong feelings against violence. The Reverend Martin Luther King Jr. was murdered.

James cried when he heard the news. When there were riots in black neighborhoods all over the country and blacks died and federal troops had to be brought in to restore order, he cried again. "To hate," James said, "to be violent, is demeaning."[20]

That had been Dr. King's conviction. It was James's conviction too.

TEN

"Precious Lord, Take My Hand"

etween the killing of Malcolm X and the murder of Martin Luther King Jr., James had begun work on a first rough draft for a film about Malcolm. It seemed important to him that a movie demonstrating how and why Malcolm had become so antiwhite and militant would be educational for white people. And it might be equally important to show black youth how Malcolm, before his death, had stopped being antiwhite without giving up the fierceness of his struggle for black rights.

In the period before he was killed, Malcolm had written his autobiography with the help of Alex Haley, who would later write the best-seller *Roots*. In early 1968, movie rights to *The Autobiography of Malcolm X* were bought by Columbia Pictures. James was asked to do the screenplay.

He traveled to Hollywood and while he was there looked up Stokely Carmichael. Carmichael had recently left SNCC to become prime minister of the Black Panther Party. James also met with other Panther leaders, including Bobby Seale, Huey Newton, and Eldridge Cleaver, who had written about him so cruelly. Understandably, while James hit it off with Seale and Newton, he and Cleaver clashed.

On the whole, James supported the work of the Panthers, which included a feeding program for children. He agreed with most of their charges against the white establishment, but not with some of their more violent statements, and he backed off from their methods, which included carrying loaded guns. When some of them faced arrest or went to jail, he spoke at meetings to raise money for their defense funds. James stood by them even when people in Hollywood who regarded them as dangerous and Communist-influenced tried to pressure him to back off.

In fact the Panthers did agree with Karl Marx that the wealth of the rich should be shared with the poor. But according to David Leeming, Baldwin "was never a believer in ideology, and he had no sympathy for the Panthers' Marxist argument. What he did believe was that the economic system of the West had no room for the people whose lives were marred by poverty and oppression."[1] James thought that had to change.

James's association with the Panthers surely shaped the attitude of the Hollywood executives toward him. As the foremost black writer in America, he had been their first choice to do the *Malcolm* script. Now it seemed he was *too* sympathetic to his subject.

From the start there were battles between Columbia and James over the screenplay. As James saw it, they wanted a softer, gentler Malcolm, a whiter—or at least a whitened—Malcolm. James felt that his screenplay was succeeding in capturing the real Malcolm, his militancy and his martyrdom. He hoped to "change this town" so that America would see the real Malcolm, and by doing this to change America.[2]

While James was writing the screenplay and arguing with Columbia, the Panthers were raided by the police, and some of them were killed. Outraged, James vowed not to let the studio force him to alter the script to misrepresent Malcolm's militancy and the reasons for it. He saw himself as "the custodian of a legend," and he was determined to write the script "my way or not at all."[3]

Nevertheless, Columbia forced a cowriter on him. This was Arnold Perl, an acquaintance whom James himself had recommended for the job. They got along well, but James's conflict with the studio continued.

Eventually, James and Columbia parted company. More than twenty years later, the two-hundred-page treatment James and Perl had produced would be the basis for Spike Lee's film on Malcolm. The film would be surrounded by controversy just as James's screenplay had been.

**Baldwin's treatment of Malcolm X would later
inspire Spike Lee's making of the movie in 1993.
Denzel Washington starred as Malcolm X.**

After the trouble over the screenplay, James went back to Europe
to regroup. He met Beauford Delaney in Paris, and they took an ex-
tended trip throughout Europe. Finally they settled down in an apartment in Istanbul, Turkey, where James worked on his writing.

In September 1971, some Black Panthers were strip-searched by
Philadelphia police and a French newspaper published a picture show-
ing them naked. James was furious. He went home to speak out at a series of meetings in defense of the Panthers.

When he returned to Europe, he had passport troubles with both
French and Turkish authorities. However, he was too well known for
them to deny him permission to reenter their countries. James continued to speak out during the next few years. While there was often official disapproval, no action was taken against him.

When *If Beale Street Could Talk* was published in 1974, its portrayal of the treatment of blacks in American jails was an embarrassment to the United States. Book reviewers, however, heaped praise on the novel. The success brought James renewed attention, and now when he spoke out against white bigotry in America his remarks were much more widely circulated.

In 1976, James gave a lecture at Bowling Green State University in Ohio. It led to an offer to teach there. When James accepted the position, it amounted to a major change in his life and lifestyle. It marked the beginning of what James Baldwin would call his "second career."[4]

During the late 1970s and early 1980s James taught at several colleges and universities. Besides Bowling Green, these included Morehouse College in Atlanta, the University of California at Berkeley, and Hampshire College and the University of Massachusetts in Amherst, Massachusetts. He taught graduate and undergraduate courses in literature and creative writing and according to his biographer James Campbell was "hugely popular on the personal level."[5] This was the result of an approach to teaching that was direct, never avoided the most touchy issues, and was related to his own personal experiences as well as to those of his students.

His message had not just to do with his students' writing, but with their lives. "Be better than you are," James would urge them. "Attempt the impossible."[6]

Everywhere he taught, James attracted a following of faculty and students, white and black, male and female, with whom he associated outside the classroom. He would preside over all-night sessions discussing modern writing, current events, history, race, sexuality, morality, and other topics. On the campus James was a father figure who challenged his students' ideas, but who was there for them when they needed him. Years later some of them would remember how they had confided privately to James about problems involving love affairs, family battles, health, and money, and how he had kept their secrets and advised them and helped them.

James related to his students in much the same way that Beauford Delaney had related to him when he was a young man. He tried to give them the same sort of understanding and support that he felt had helped him escape the inner city and freed him to become a writer. Delaney had been a major influence in his life, and when James received news that he had died in Paris on March 26, 1979, he could not be consoled. The grief James kept "bottled up inside" made him physically ill, and for a while he couldn't meet his teaching commitments.[7]

At this time James had just completed the novel he had been working on for three years called *Just Above My Head*. It was a long novel divided into six "Books." Parts of it were based on James's life, and some of the characters were based on people he had known. He had deliberately written the dialogue with a jazz or blues beat. The book reinvolved James in an argument that had begun almost twenty-five years earlier at Howard University. Much of *Just Above My Head* was written in Black English.

Black English was as controversial in 1979 as it had been back in 1955. In July 1979, James tackled the subject head-on in a *New York*

In 1979, an older Baldwin finished *Just Above My Head*.

Times op-ed column titled "If Black English Isn't a Language, Then Tell Me, What Is?" He wrote that "people evolve a language" so they won't be drowned by a reality they can't put into words. He called Black English "a political instrument" and "the most crucial key to identity." He argued that it had come about because of a "brutal necessity" to communicate an African-American pain that was outside the bounds of ordinary English.[8] He insisted that Black English was as legitimate a form of language as any other.

Book reviewers became involved in the dispute when *Just Above My Head* was published. Much of their criticism had to do with that aspect of the novel. But they also found fault with its bulk, its structure, its lack of depth, and its characterizations. Baldwin himself had perhaps best defined the novel in a short story he had written many years before called "Sonny's Blues," in which he declared, "While the tale of how we suffer, and how we are delighted, and how we may triumph is never new, it always must be heard. There isn't any other tale to tell; it's the only light we've got in all the darkness."[9]

As the years passed, James continued to speak out against bigotry and for tolerance. At the University of Florida in the spring of 1980, James took part in a dialogue with the acclaimed Nigerian novelist Chinua Achebe. As James was talking, there were crackling noises on the speakers. Somehow a shortwave radio operator had cut into the transmission from the speakers' microphones. "You gonna have to cut it out, Mr. Baldwin," he threatened clearly and loudly. "We can't stand for this kind of going on."[10] The threats continued, but the crackling kept the words from being understood.

James shouted back over the crackling in a firm and steady voice. "Mr. Baldwin is nevertheless going to finish his statement!" he announced, adding, "If you assassinate me in the next two minutes I'm telling you this: it no longer matters what you think. The doctrine of white supremacy . . . has had its hour, has had its day—it's over!"[11]

The incident was not the only reason James had his doubts about racial harmony in what was then being called the New South. That same year he had covered a trial for *Esquire* magazine in Birmingham, Alabama. He had watched a white man accused of throwing a bomb into a black church go "free as lightning" into a white world where men "wore their Ku Klux Klan insignias on the sidebars of their eyeglasses."[12]

What really convinced James that the New South had a long way to go when it came to race relations was the case of the Atlanta child murders. There had been twenty-eight murders of black children in Atlanta between 1979 and 1982. For a long time the police were unable to come up with a suspect.

In early 1981, James traveled to Atlanta to do a story about the child murders for *Playboy*. He found a black community convinced that if the victims had been white children, the police would have already taken steps to stop the murders. Atlanta blacks believed there was a good chance the killer was white and they suspected a cover-up. James too became persuaded that the authorities were dragging their feet. In June, however, a twenty-three-year-old black man named Wayne Williams was arrested and charged with the crime although police could implicate him in only two of the twenty-eight deaths.

James's article on the Atlanta child murders appeared in the December 1981 issue of *Playboy* under the title "The Evidence of Things Not Seen." Later it would win the magazine's Best Nonfiction Award for that year. But that would not end James's involvement with the case.

He continued to follow the nine-week trial of Williams, who was convicted by a jury after only twelve hours of deliberations. When the sentence of two consecutive life terms was imposed, the mother of one of the victims said a "kangaroo court put Wayne Williams in jail and a killer on the streets."[13] James too was unconvinced that Williams was responsible for all twenty-eight black children's deaths. He began work on a book about the case which would be an expansion of the *Playboy* article.

James went to France to work on the book version of *The Evidence of Things Not Seen*. During the following months he also worked on some poems he had written over the years, rewriting and polishing them, and jotting down a few new ones. James looked at poetry as "my way of experimenting" with Black English.[14] The poems were published under the title *Jimmy's Blues* in London in 1983.

On May 4 of that year, James finished writing *The Evidence of Things Not Seen*. But as James would again learn, writing a book and getting it published are not the same thing. Several American publishing houses turned down *The Evidence of Things Not Seen.* In their opinion, Baldwin did not appreciate the sweeping changes in the New South and had a warped view of the Atlanta child murder cases. Among those who turned the book down was Dial Press, which had been publishing James for almost thirty years.

James was sure that politics were behind the rejections. He believed that a New South was necessary to white America's selling itself to the world. The oppression of black people was not good for business, so they would no longer be oppressed. Except that many still were.

The Evidence of Things Not Seen was published in both France and England before the American publisher Henry Holt brought it out in 1986. Between the time it was written and the time it became available to American readers, James had returned to America. In September 1983, he began teaching at Hampshire College and the University of Massachusetts in Amherst, Massachusetts.

The pressures of lecturing and teaching and writing began telling on James's health. In the summer of 1983 he had had a minor heart attack. Now, in the fall of 1984 he was again hospitalized for heart problems. Following his release from the hospital he was given an official sixtieth birthday party at the University of Massachusetts. African-American poet Maya Angelou paid tribute to James with a speech from the heart about his life and work.

Despite ill health, during 1985 James began work on a book tentatively titled *Remember This House.* It was to be a testimonial to the three slain black leaders Medgar Evers, Malcolm X, and Dr. Martin Luther King Jr. James worked on it on and off through that year and into the next.

In June 1986, James went to France to receive the French Legion of Honor from President François Mitterrand. In October, along with playwright Arthur Miller and writer-actor Peter Ustinov, he journeyed to a conference in the Soviet Union where he delivered a speech on how racism destroyed the racist as well as the victim.

As he always had, James was pushing himself too hard. He spent long hours working on *Remember This House.* His involvement in world politics continued. But he was not feeling well at all. He had frequent

**Baldwin and Leonard Bernstein proudly pose
with the French Legion of Honor.**

stomach discomfort and the pains became worse and worse. They were finally diagnosed as cancer of the esophagus. On April 25, 1987, an operation was performed. James went to his house in Saint Paul de Vence in France to convalesce. But the operation had been too late. The cancer had spread.

He continued trying to work on *Remember This House*. But his strength failed him and it would never be finished. He was very sick now, and family members and old friends came to visit him. Among them were his brother David and his former lover Lucien. They were at his bedside on December 1, 1987, when James Baldwin passed away.

The funeral service was held in New York City at the Cathedral of St. John the Divine. Traditional psalms were sung and jazz improvisations were played. The King James Bible was read from in old English

James Baldwin

Baldwin spent his last years trying to complete *Remember This House*.

and eulogies were delivered in Black English. The highlight of the service was a tape of James himself singing the hymn "Precious Lord, Take My Hand, Lead Me On." With the sound of his voice it was as if he was there.

A black man had died and the movement had lost a witness. A man who loved men had died and gays had lost a pioneer. An American had died and the country had lost a writer.

He had written that "The terms of our Revolution—the American Revolution—are these: not that I drive you out or that you drive me out, but that we learn to live together."[15]

That was always the message of James Baldwin. There could be no more fitting epitaph.

Source Notes

Chapter One

1. James Baldwin, *The Devil Finds Work* (New York: Dial, 1976), p. 7.
2. James Baldwin, *Go Tell It on the Mountain* (New York: Dell, 1985), p. 19.
3. David Leeming, *James Baldwin* (New York: Alfred A. Knopf, 1994), p. 20.
4. James Baldwin, *The Fire Next Time* (New York: Vintage, 1993), p. 74.
5. Ibid., p. 94.
6. Ibid., p. 105.
7. Ibid., p. 88.
8. Ibid., p. 83.
9. Leeming, p. 172.
10. Ibid., p. 172
11. *The Fire Next Time*, p. 91.

Chapter Two

1. James Baldwin, *Go Tell It on the Mountain* (New York: Dell, 1985), p. 166.

2. David Leeming, *James Baldwin* (New York: Alfred A. Knopf, 1994), p. 4.
3. James Campbell, *Talking at the Gates: A Life of James Baldwin* (New York: Viking, 1991), p. 4.
4. James Baldwin, *The Devil Finds Work* (New York: Dial, 1976), pp. 13–14.
5. Leeming, p. 16.
6. Ibid., p. 16.
7. James Baldwin, *Notes of a Native Son* (Boston: Beacon Press, 1984) p. 3.
8. Lisa Rosset, *James Baldwin* (Los Angeles: Melrose Square, 1990) pp. 29–30.
9. James M. McPherson, *Battle Cry of Freedom: The Civil War Era* (New York: Oxford University Press, 1988) p. 90.
10. *Go Tell It on the Mountain*, p. 37.
11. Ibid., p. 37.
12. James Baldwin, *National Coalition Against Censorship* letter (New York, 1995) p. 1.
13. Campbell, p. 16
14. James Baldwin letter to Langston Hughes, March 25, 1953.
15. Faith Berry, *Langston Hughes: Before and Beyond Harlem* (Westport, Conn.: Lawrence Hill & Company, 1983), p. 43.
16. Leeming, p. 26.
17. *National Review*, August 13, 1963.
18. Rosset, p. 47.
19. James Baldwin, *The Fire Next Time* (New York: Vintage, 1993), p. 40.
20. Leeming, p. 31.
21. *The Fire Next Time*, p. 41.
22. *Notes of a Native Son*, p. xv.

Chapter Three

1. James Baldwin, *Notes of a Native Son* (Boston: Beacon Press, 1984). p. 94.
2. David Leeming, *James Baldwin* (New York: Alfred A. Knopf, 1994), p. 39.
3. Baldwin, p. 93.

4. Ibid., pp. 93–94.
5. Ibid., pp. 95–97.
6. Ibid., pp. 98–99.
7. Ibid., p. 111.
8. James Baldwin, *Another Country* (New York: Dial, 1962), p. 3.
9. *Encyclopaedia Britannica*, Book X, 1984, p. 762.
10. James Baldwin, *The Devil Finds Work* (New York: Dial, 1976), p. 33.
11. James Campbell, *Talking at the Gates: A Life of James Baldwin* (New York: Viking, 1991), p. 22.
12. James Baldwin, *Nobody Knows My Name* (New York: Dell, 1988), p. 153.
13. Ibid., p. 154.
14. Campbell, p. 32.
15. *Another Country,* p. 87.
16. Ibid,. pp. 87–88.
17. Campbell, p. 38.
18. Ibid., p. 38.
19. *New Leader,* April 10, 1948.
20. Ibid.
21. *Notes of a Native Son,* pp. 71–72.
22. Campbell, p. 42.

Chapter Four

1. David Leeming, *James Baldwin* (New York: Alfred A. Knopf, 1994), p. 57.
2. Ibid., p. 59.
3. James Campbell, *Talking at the Gates: A Life of James Baldwin* (New York: Viking, 1991), p. 52.
4. Leeming, p. 60.
5. *Partisan Review,* June 1949.
6. Lisa Rosset, *James Baldwin* (Los Angeles: Melrose Square, 1990) p. 72.
7. Leeming, p. 64.
8. Campbell, p. 57.
9. Ibid., p. 58.
10. *Harper's,* March 1945.

11. James Baldwin, *Notes of a Native Son* (Boston: Beacon Press, 1984), p. 143.
12. Ibid., p. 143.
13. *Harper's*, March 1945
14. Baldwin, p. 158.

Chapter Five

1. James Baldwin, *Giovanni's Room* (New York: Dell, 1988), p. 32.
2. Ibid., p. 59.
3. David Leeming, *James Baldwin* (New York: Alfred A. Knopf, 1994), pp. 74–75.
4. James Campbell, *Talking at the Gates: A Life of James Baldwin* (New York: Viking, 1991), p. 61.
5. James Baldwin, *Notes of a Native Son* (Boston: Beacon Press, 1984) p. 161.
6. James Baldwin, *Nobody Knows My Name* (New York: Dell, 1988), p. 88.
7. Campbell, p. 61.
8. Ibid., p. 61.
9. Leeming, pp. 74–75.
10. Leeming, p. 89.
11. Leeming, p. 90.
12. *Chronicles of the 20th Century* (Mount Kisco, NY: Chronicle Publications, 1987), p. 753.
13. Campbell, pp. 90–91.
14. Ibid., pp.90–91.
15. Leeming, p. 110.
16. *Notes of a Native Son*, p. 175.
17. *New York Times Book Review*, 28 Feb. 1956.
18. Leeming, pp. 128–129.
19. Ibid., p. 125.

Chapter Six

1. James Baldwin, *Nobody Knows My Name* (New York: Dell, 1988), p. 64.

2. David Leeming, *James Baldwin* (New York: Alfred A. Knopf, 1994), p. 116.
3. Harold Isaacs, "Five Writers and Their Ancestors" (*Phylon* magazine, Winter, 1960).
4. *Chronicles of the 20th Century* (Mount Kisco, N. Y.: Chronicle Publications, 1987), p. 778.
5. Baldwin, p. 75.
6. *Chronicles of the 20th Century*, p. 805.
7. Ibid., p805.
8. Baldwin, p. 90.
9. Ibid., p. 90
10. Ibid., p. 90.
11. Ibid., p. 93.
12. Lisa Rosset, *James Baldwin* (Los Angeles: Melrose Square, 1990), p. 93.

Chapter Seven

1. James Baldwin, *Nobody Knows My Name* (New York: Dell, 1988), p. 64.
2. Ibid., p. 62.
3. Ibid., p. 66.
4. Ibid., p. 59.
5. Ibid., p. 64.
6. Ibid., p. 64.
7. Ibid., p. 65.
8. James Campbell, *Talking at the Gates: A Life of James Baldwin* (New York: Viking, 1991), p. 157.
9. Ibid., p. 154.
10. Ibid., p. 157
11. Ibid., p. 157.
12. *New York Times Book Review*, Dec. 2, 1962.
13. David Leeming, *James Baldwin* (New York: Alfred A. Knopf, 1994), p. 200.
14. Campbell, p. 158.

Chapter Eight

1. Ted Gottfried, *Malcolm X* (Prince Frederick, Md: Recorded Books, Inc., 1994), p. 13.
2. James Campbell, *Talking at the Gates: A Life of James Baldwin* (New York: Viking, 1991), p. 161.
3. Gottfried, p. 18.
4. James Baldwin, *The Fire Next Time* (New York: Vintage, 1993), p. 45.
5. Ibid., p. 48.
6. Ibid., pp. 63–64.
7. Ibid., p. 65.
8. Ibid., p. 71.
9. Campbell, p. 160.
10. Lisa Rosset, *James Baldwin* (Los Angeles: Melrose Square, 1990), p. 116.
11. Ibid., p. 898.
12. Gottfried, p. 19.
13. Ibid., p. 19.
14. Campbell, p. 176.
15. James Baldwin, *If Beale Street Could Talk* (New York: Dial, 1974), p. 65.

Chapter Nine

1. *Current Biography* 1964, p. 24.
2. David Leeming, *James Baldwin* (New York: Alfred A. Knopf, 1994), p. 237
3. Ibid., p. 237.
4. *Chronicles of the 20th Century* (Mount Kisco, N. Y.: Chronicle Publications, 1987), p. 913.
5. Ibid., p. 919.
6. Leeming, p. 256.
7. James Campbell, *Talking at the Gates: A Life of James Baldwin* (New York: Viking, 1991), p. 207.
8. Leeming, p. 256.

9. James Baldwin, *The Fire Next Time* (New York: Vintage, 1993), p. 5.
10. *Encyclopaedia Britannica*, Book 11, 1984, p. 110.
11. Baldwin, p. 106.
12. Campbell, p. 217.
13. Lyric, "We Shall Overcome."
14. Stephen B. Oates, *Let the Trumpet Sound: The Life of Martin Luther King, Jr.*(New York: Harper & Row, 1982), pp. 386–387.
15. Ibid., pp. 386–7
16. Leeming, p. 257.
17. Lisa Rosset, *James Baldwin* (Los Angeles: Melrose Square, 1990), p. 147.
18. Ibid., p. 149.
19. *The Nation,* July 11, 1966.
20. Rosset, p. 152.

Chapter Ten

1. David Leeming, *James Baldwin* (New York: Alfred A. Knopf, 1994), p. 294.
2. James Baldwin letter to David Baldwin, March 10, 1968.
3. *Cinema 4* magazine, Summer, 1968.
4. Leeming, p. 336.
5. James Campbell, *Talking at the Gates: A Life of James Baldwin* (New York: Viking, 1991), p. 274.
6. Leeming, p. 340.
7. Ibid., p. 341.
8. James Baldwin, *New York Times* Op–Ed page, July 29, 1979.
9. Leeming, p. 349.
10. Campbell, p. 279.
11. Ibid., p. 279.
12. *Esquire* magazine, October 1980.
13. *Chronicles of the 20th Century* (Mount Kisco, N. Y.: Chronicle Publications, 1987), p. 1200.
14. Leeming, p. 360.
15. Lisa Rosset, *James Baldwin* (Los Angeles: Melrose Square, 1990), p. 167.

Books by
JAMES BALDWIN

(Listed in order of original publication)

Go Tell It on the Mountain. New York: Dell, 1985. An autobiographical novel about growing up in Harlem as a preacher's son.

Notes of a Native Son. Boston: Beacon Press, 1984. A collection of articles ranging from "The Harlem Ghetto" to "The Negro in Paris."

Giovanni's Room. New York: Dell, 1988. Fiction; love between a man who backs away from being gay and one who accepts his feelings.

Nobody Knows My Name. New York: Dell, 1988. Essays, including profiles of writers Norman Mailer and Richard Wright and film director Ingmar Bergman.

Another Country. New York: Dial, 1962. A novel set in Manhattan about relationships among gays and straights, blacks and whites, down-and-out artists and successful performers.

The Fire Next Time. New York: Vintage, 1993. A nonfiction work that takes off from an interview with the leader of the Black Muslims to consider the hatred of blacks for whites. It was a wake-up call for America when it was written in the 1960s, and its message may be even more urgent today.

Books by James Baldwin

Blues for Mister Charlie. New York: Dial, 1964. A play based on the real-life case of a Northern African-American teenager lynched in the South for flirting with a white woman.

Going to Meet the Man New York: Dial, 1965. A collection of short stories dealing with race and other matters.

The Amen Corner. New York: Dial, 1968. A play about church life in Harlem.

Tell Me How Long the Train's Been Gone. New York: Dial, 1968. A novel about the problems of a black actor in a white society.

A Rap on Race (with Margaret Mead). Philadelphia: Lippincott, 1971. Conversations with a noted anthropologist about race and prejudice.

If Beale Street Could Talk. New York: Dial, 1974. A moving novel about a black family's search for evidence to free a young sculptor who has been wrongly jailed.

The Devil Finds Work. New York: Dial, 1976. Racism in movies, and some notable exceptions to it.

Just Above My Head. New York: Dial, 1979. A novel about blacks and whites with much of the writing in Black English.

Jimmy's Blues: Selected Poems. New York: St. Martin's, 1985. Written over many years, these poems are like a tenor saxophone blowing lonely riffs late at night.

The Evidence of Things Not Seen. New York: Holt, Rinehart and Winston, 1985. An analysis of the Atlanta child murders and the trial of the man convicted of them.

SUGGESTED FURTHER READING

Bode, Janet. *Different Worlds: Inter-Racial and Cross-Cultural Dating.* New York: Franklin Watts, 1989. Problems and rewards of young people who try to live up to Baldwin's love-based beliefs.

Brown, Kevin. *Malcolm X: His Life and Legacy.* Brookfield, Conn: Millbrook, 1995. The man and the myth with excerpts from speeches and TV interviews.

Campbell, James. *Talking at the Gates: A Life of James Baldwin.* New York: Viking, 1991. A critical examination of Baldwin's work and life.

Leeming, David. *James Baldwin.* New York: Alfred A. Knopf, 1994. A biography as told by one who worked and lived with Baldwin during the last years of his life.

Rosset, Lisa. *James Baldwin.* Los Angeles: Melrose Square, 1990. A well-written account for young adults of Baldwin's childhood, civil rights activities and writings.

Steptoe, Michele. *African-American Voices.* (Brookfield, Conn: Millbrook, 1995. A varied collection of writings by black journalists, poets, and novelists.

Index

Italicized page numbers refer to photos

Amen Corner, The (play), 24, 51, 52
Anderson, Marian, 55
Angelou, Maya, 96
Another Country, 32-33, 36-37, 64,
    66–68
Atlanta child murders, 95–96
Avedon, Richard, 25

Back to Africa movement, 70
Baldwin, David (step-father), 9,
    17–18, 19, 23, 24, 26, 29, 30,
    31, 32, 33, 48
Baldwin, David (brother), 80, 97
Baldwin, Emma Berdis Jones
    (mother), 9, 15–16, 17, 18, 19,
    30, 33, 40
Baldwin, James, *10, 25, 65, 77, 78, 93,*
    97, 98
    awards, 36, 40, 53, 95, 96
    birth, 9, 15, 17
    and Black Panthers, 86–87,
        89–90, 91
    childhood, 9–10, 17–27

    as child preacher, 24–25, 26, 27, 51
    and civil rights movement,
        11–13, 51, 52–53, 57–63,
        64–66, 68, 76–77, 80, 81,
        83, 84, 98
    death, 97–98
    education, 18, 22–27
    essays and articles, 12–13,
        19–20, 29, 38, 39, 41–43,
        48, 49, 50, 52–53, 58,
        61–63, 64–66, 69, 70–75,
        81, 85, 94, 95–97
    and Malcolm X screenplay,
        89–90, 91
    and Nation of Islam, 12, 70,
        71–75
    novels, 10, 32–33, 34, 36–37,
        46–47, 48, 49, 50, 51, 52,
        53–54, 55, 64, 66–68, 79,
        92, 93–94
    in Paris, 40–47, 48, 50, 58, 91
    plays, 24, 50, 51, 52, 56, 80–81
    poetry, 23–24, 95

as reviewer, 37–38, 41–42
sexuality, 10, 27, 34, 53–54, 74
short stories, 38–39, 86–87, 94
as teacher, 92–93
opposition to Vietnam War,
    82–83, 84
Baldwin, Paula (sister), 30
Baldwin, Samuel (half-brother), 17,
    19
Baldwin, Wilmer (brother), 48
Baraka, Amiri, 81, 86
Belafonte, Harry, 76
Berry, Faith, 24
Birmingham, Alabama, 66, 76,
    77–78, 80, 94–95
Black English, 52, 93–94, 95
"Black Girl Shouting" (poem),
    23–24
Black Muslims, 12, 13, 70, 72, 73,
    74, 75, 76, 83
Black Nationalist Party, 81
Black Panther Party, 86, 89–90, 91
Blues for Mister Charlie (play), 56,
    80–81
Brando, Marlon, 34, 48, 77

Capote, Truman, 41, *42*
Capouya, Emile, 25, 26, 29
Carmichael, Stokely, 86, *87* 89
Chaney, James, 84
Charlotte, North Carolina, 58, 60
Civil rights movement, 11–13, 51,
    55–63, 64, 68–69, 73, 75,
    76–79, 81, 83–86, 98
Clark, Kenneth, 76
Cleaver, Eldridge, 86, 89
Congress of Racial Equality
    (CORE), 68, 86
Counts, Dorothy, 60
Cullen, Countee, 23, 24

Deal Island, Maryland, 15

Delaney, Beauford, 26–27, 29, 32,
    33, 50, 91, 92–93
DeWitt Clinton High School, 24,
    25, 26, 27

Eugene F. Saxton Foundation
    Fellowship, 36
Evers, Medgar, 75, 80, 96
"Everybody's Protest Novel"
    (essay), 41–42
"Evidence of Things Not Seen,
    The" (essay), 95
Evidence of Things Not Seen, The,
    95–96

Fard, Wallace, 70
Federal Bureau of Investigations
    (FBI), 68–69
"Fifth Avenue Uptown: A Letter
    from Harlem" (essay), 64–66
"Fire Next Time, The" (essay),
    70–71, 74
Fire Next Time, The, 12–13, 20, 69,
    70, 71–75, 81, 85
France, 53, 58, 60, 96. *See also* Paris,
    France
Frederick Douglass Junior High
    School, 22, 23

Gandhi, Mohandas K., 61
Garvey, Marcus, 70
Giovanni's Room, 11, 46–47, 50, 52,
    53–54, 55
Going to Meet The Man, 86–87
Goodman, Andrew, 84
Go Tell It on the Mountain 10, 34, 36,
    47, 48, 49, 50, 51
Greenwich Village, New York City,
    26, 29, 33–34, 38, 39, 66

Haley, Alex, 89
Hansberry, Lorraine, 76

Index

Happersberger, Lucien, 46–47, 53, 97
Harlem, New York City, 11, 16–17, 16, 24, 26, 28, 29, 33, 9, 40, 51, 52, 64–66, 73, 83
    riot, 30–32, 31
"Harlem Ghetto, The" (essay), 38, 39
Harlem Renaissance, 16, 28
Hoetis, Themistocles, 51
Homosexuality, 10, 11, 13, 27, 33, 34, 53–54, 66, 74
Hoover, J. Edgar, 68–69
Horn, Bishop Rosa Artemis, 24, 51
Horne, Lena, 76
Howard University Players, 52
Hughes, Langston, 17, 24, 53, 67
Hurston, Zora Neale, 17

If Beale Street Could Talk, 79, 92
"If Black English Isn't a Language, Then Tell Me, What Is?" (essay), 94

Jimmy's Blues (poetry), 95
Julian Rosenwald Foundation, 40
Just Above My Head, 93–94

Kennedy, Robert, 76
King, Martin Luther, Jr., 56, 57, 58, 61–62, 62, 68–69, 72, 76, 77, 81, 83, 84, 86, 88, 89, 96
Knopf, Alfred, 48, 51, 53
Ku Klux Klan, 16, 76, 95

Lee, Canada, 34, 35
Lee, Spike, 90
Leeming, David, 50, 57, 84, 90
Little Rock, Arkansas, 59–60, 66
Liuzzo, Viola, 84
Lockridge, Ross, 38
Loeche-les-Bains, Switzerland, 47, 48, 49
Lucy, Autherine, 58

McKissick, Floyd, 86
Mailer, Norman, 67
Malcolm X, 12, 34, 72, 72, 74–75, 76, 77, 78, 79, 80, 81, 3, 89, 90, 96
March on Washington (1963), 77
Meredith, James, 71, 86
Miller, Orilla, 18–19
Milliam, J.W., 56
Montgomery bus boycott, 56–57, 61–62
Muhammad, Elijah, 12, 70, 71, 72, 73, 74, 75

National Association for the Advancement of Colored People (NAACP), 75
National Institute of Arts and Letters, 53
Nation of Islam, 70, 71–75, 76, 81
Native Son (Wright), 34, 41–42
"Negro in Paris, The" (essay), 42–43
New Jersey, 29–30, 33, 37
Newton, Huey, 89
New York City, 11, 16, 28, 44, 66, 83, 87, 97
Nobody Knows My Name, 48, 66
Notes of a Native Son, 19–20, 29, 52–53

Paris, France, 11, 40, 46, 47, 48, 50, 58, 91, 93
Parks, Rosa, 56, 57
Pelatowski, Theodore, 40
Perl, Arnold, 90
Porter, Herman, 22–23
"Previous Condition" (short story), 39

Race riots, 13, 30–32, 38, 81, 85, 87, 88

Reeb, James, 84
Remember This House, 96–97
Robeson, Paul, 34
Russell, Bertrand, 82

Sartre, Jean-Paul, 41, *43*
Schwerner, Michael, 84
Seale, Bobby, 89
Segregation, 9, 12, 16, 28, 48, 50–51, 55, 56, 58, 59–61, 66, 76
Selma, Alabama, 81–82, 83–84
"Sonny's Blues" (short story), 94
Southern Christian Leadership Conference (SCLC), 61, 68
Student Nonviolent Coordinating Committee (SNCC), 68, 86, 89

Till, Emmett, 55–56, 80

Uncle Tom's Cabin (Stowe), 20, *21*, 41
University of Mississippi, 70, 86
Up From Slavery (Washington), 20

Vietnam War, 82–83, 84

Watts riots, 13, 85
White Citizens Councils, 58, 76
Williams, Wayne, 95
Worth, Eugene, 36–37
Wright, Richard, 34–36, *35*, 41–42, 49